AF507300

Beyond the
Power Lines

E. Reid Gilbert

A3D Impressions

Tucson / Minneapolis

MEMOIRS

E. Reid Gilbert

Beyond the Power Lines Where the Pavement Ends

A3D Impressions

Tucson / Minneapolis

Published by

A3D Impressions
P.O. Box 14181, Tucson, AZ 85732
www.a3dimpressions.com
a3dimpressions@gmail.com

Publisher's Cataloging-in-Publication data

Names: Gilbert, E. Reid, author.
Title: Beyond the power lines / E. Reid Gilbert.
Description: Tucson, AZ; Minneapolis, MN: A3D Impressions, 2022.
Identifiers: LCCN: 2022912383 | ISBN: 979-8-9864049-0-5
Subjects: LCSH American poetry--21st century. | Grief--Poetry. | Essays.
| BISAC POETRY / General POETRY / American / General | POETRY
/ Subjects & Themes / Death, Grief, Loss | POETRY / Subjects &
Themes / Places
Classification: LCC PS3607 .I42243 B49 2022 | DDC 811.6

Special thanks to Judith Holt
for assistance in editing.

Contents

—————————————————————)(————————————————

Paved Roads

We moved to Baux Mountain in October, 1939. I carved the date on a smooth bark maple just below the future chicken house site and above a wet weather spring.

On the moving-in day, sister Susie (Della Sue), aged 11, little brother Ott (Arthur Brinkley), aged six, and I, almost nine, decided to take a hike in the nearby woods. Actually, to be perfectly honest about it, I persuaded them to go with me and investigate our new woods. I also felt that we were probably in the way of the folks carrying things into the house. Herman Murphy had used his truck and lent a hand, also with Gil Easter helping.

As soon as we were in the woods and out of sight of the house, we could hear water trickling. Two small branches of water came together just above the four-foot rock escarpment, we had discovered a waterfall.

We took our shoes and socks off and waded in the little pool below the falls. After a bit of fun in the water, splashing ourselves with the cool spring water, I suggested, "We might find some-thing even bigger, if we go down the branch a little farther."

They agreed as we carried our shoes and splashed our way down the thin stream of water. But, sure enough, several yards down the branch, we stood on the top of a set of stairs. At least they looked like stairsteps of rock imbedded together like stacked bricks. The steps ended about 30 feet down at the edge of a pool, larger than the one we had enjoyed upstream.

It was great fun walking up and down the stair steps, pretending all sorts of things like Indians, ancient warriors, royalty. A large tree stump at the top of the steps served an appropriate royal throne.

However, the time seemed to pass too quickly, as the light began to fade. We were at the north-eastern base of Baux Mountain, and the sun was beginning its decline.

I said, "We'd better get back. It's getting late and Mamma and Daddy don't know where we are."

"Now Reid, how can they know where we are, when we don't know where we are."

"Oh, I know."

"Tell us then, so we can know. Where are we?"

"We're in the dark woods."

"Silly, we know that, but how are they gonna find us if we can't find our way back."

We were lost, but I dared not panic, as they were already scared. So I had to put on a demeanor of adventure, while my heart palpitations were bombarding my rib cage.

"Reid, are you sure you know what you're doing?," asked sister Susie.

"Of course, I know." Lying through my teeth.

"Don't you think it's time to get back to our new house?"

I had been trying for the past hour to figure out, in the midst of our playing, where we really were. Then the question was how to leave that spot and get back to the house and the folks.

Climbing up the branch bank, we, all three, were getting black soot over our arms, faces and clothes from burnt-out tree logs. We had been told that there had been a huge forest fire in the woods the year before the folks bought the place.

"Now, I believe that if we go up this hill we'll be there."

"What makes you think that?"

"Don't you remember we came down a hill?"

"Yes!"

"Well!"

"Eddie Reid, how do you know it's the same hill?"

When she addressed me that way, I knew she was serious and getting angry. And you didn't want to be close by when Susie would get really upset. 'Cause then she'd begin to cuss, and the four-letter words she'd use were DARN IT, DRAT THE DADBLAMED THING, DADBURN IT ANYWAY. But she'd use the words with such feeling that she sounded like a sailor swearing. She hadn't started cussin' yet, but I didn't answer her. I just started climbing the hill.

"Ott stay close now," as I pulled him up a steep incline. "You coming too, Susie or are you wantin' to sleep here tonight with the bears?"

"The bears?" As she started climbin' and crawlin' faster to catch up. The mention of bears seemed to provide extra motivation to quit talking and speed up her climbing pace.

Shortly we began to see beyond the trees to light, which I supposed was an open field. "See? We're nearly back. The light up there!"

"How do we know it's the light at the house?"

"C'mon! Let's see!"

Three dirty urchins burst through underbrush into an open field and into the late afternoon sunlight.

Susie was right. We were out of the woods, but in a strange place that we had not seen before. "Well, Mr. Explorer, where's the house? Well, tell us now where is it?"

"They musta moved it."

"Smartypants, don't ..."

Ott piped up, "Susie, could they move a big ... ?"

"Of course they couldn't, an' they didn't. We're more lost than we were in the woods. At least we had water in the branch to drink to keep us alive, if it takes them a long time to find us."

I was keeping my distance from her, until I made a discovery. "Look across this field and over the tops of those trees. Whatta you see?"

"I see a big old house."

"Well?"

"Well, what? It might could be where that old witch woman lives."

Ott asked again, "Is there a witch woman?"

"Maybe but that isn't where she ... if you look real good. An' listen real good, we might hear somethin'."

We heard a sound coming from the house like a kind of horn, then words, "Reid, Susie!"

"We're way over here. We'll be right there."
It didn't take us long to scamper across the field,

---

jumped over a little gully of blackberry briars and trudge through a stretch of red oak saplings to the back of our new (old) house.

Mamma was standing on the back porch above our heads. "Where have you young'uns been?"

Ott answered, "We went to see the bears."

"What bears? You know there ... and how did you get so sooty?"

Susie said, "Reid led us down the creek and across the old burnout logs."

Ott said, "An' we found a mountain an' waterfalls."

"Well your daddy just went into the house when he saw you coming up the hill. He's really upset. I'll go get him, but he'll want a full accounting of your scaring us so bad."

She went into the kitchen, and I said to Susie and also to Ott. "Now let me tell the story, 'cause if we're not real careful, Susie, you and I'll get a whipping ... an' you know what whippin's ..."

She seemed determined to tell her own version and announced to me, "I don't care if I get a whippin'. I just wanta see you get a good one." I believe we both had the opportunity to tell our own versions of the afternoon expedition. We didn't get whippings.

I had a hard time understanding the sacrifice she was willing to make to get a whipping just to see me get one. I suppose she'd enjoy seeing me dance when I'd get a switching on my bare legs.

That could be for later occasions.

————————————————)((————————————————

The Gilbert Kids

After that first day in our new place and our foray into the woods, almost lost, our relationships began to emerge. Of course, the physical locations of our activities dictated a great deal of how we would work or play. Susie was mostly confined to the house to help Mamma with the demands of such a primitive setup; no running water, no electricity, no phone.

Of course we would be with her when we'd eat and sleep in the house. And sometimes she'd venture out for one reason or another.

One reason was to use the outhouse. If Susie needed to use the outhouse after dark, I'd have to go with her and stand outside. In cold weather, I'd yell, "Hurry up, Susie. It's cold out here. "

She'd yell back, "You can't hurry up these things." The reason I'd have to go with her after dark was that she was afraid she'd encounter a bear or be bitten by a scorpion. How would I prevent her from being bitten by a scorpion was unknown. Actually there were no scorpions in the first place.

"Susie, there're no scorpions or bears here."

"You said there were bears here."

"When did I say that?"

"The first day we moved here and we got lost in the woods. You said that a bear might get me." That was true and I did say that; a truth I'd have to bear and live with.

I should describe the outhouse which was the only structure beside the house on the whole place ... no barn, no chicken house, not even a shed for a cow.

The outhouse had been built by the WPA* guys. It was much fancier than other outhouses we had used at other places. It had a concrete floor and a concrete stool, it had a lid with a screen on the top to keep blowflies out. It had a nice tin roof and german-siding planks on the outside. It was painted white ... the only paint on any wall we had (of the house). It was fancy for an outhouse.

Ott and I would often tease Susie. One day we pretended to tell a joke then laugh about it. The joke was there was an iceberg with penguins, and it was floating north. There was another iceberg with penguins floating south. When they were about to pass each other, one of the penguins yelled, "RADIO!" Then we'd both laugh. Susie said, "I don't get it."

"You know RADIO." Then we'd both laugh again, as though it was the funniest joke in the world. One day when she was barefoot, she stepped on a little green snake in the garden. She said to me "Reid , do you think I'll die?"

*Works Progress Administration

I said, "Yeah." Saying to myself that everybody's gonna die some time.

Actually, we all got along except for some teasing. When we were living with Uncle Bob, and Daddy had lost his job at Hanes Hosiery, we were so poor that Susie and I had to share a pair of shoes. She'd wear the shoes to school, and as I wasn't in school yet, I could wear them after she got home. If it was summer, of course, I'd go barefoot, not needing any shoes.

Susie was so easily frightened. One Halloween, Susie, Uncle Jack and I decided to go to the Taylors and scare the girls there. We got our stuff together and headed up the road a couple hundred yards to the Taylors.

We had a cornfield with corn shocks about half-way there. As we went by a corn shock, a white ghost started floating toward us from behind the tepee-shaped dry cornstalks. Susie ran toward the Taylors. Jack and I ran back home.

The ghost was a white sheet held in the air by Daddy. I don't know how he got there so quick, as I thought he was sitting in a chair in the kitchen when we left.

Daddy sent me to go get Susie, tell her it was Daddy and bring her home. I was unsuccessful in that assignment, so Jack had to go and fetch her home. He failed also. Daddy had to go get her.

Later on when Susie was dating, Henry Bowen (the fellow she was dating) stepped out on the running board while the car was moving. Susie said, "What are you doing?"

"You're sittin' so close you're pushing me out the door." He was teasing her, because she was clutching her door handle, so she wouldn't slide toward Henry around a curve. She was well aware of his cousin, Ruth and J. D. Perrell in the front seat when a carload of us would go to the drive-in.

Ott was the exact opposite of Susie. He was always performing. Before we moved out to Baux Mountain Ott and Susie and I would walk to Oak Summit Church for Sunday School. We'd have to walk past a country store where there would usually, in good weather, have several men sitting on a bench in front of the store. They'd offer Ott some pennies for the collection, if he'd dance for them.

He'd dance and get his pennies. Susie stood shyly to one side. I said to the men, "I can dance too." I must have been invisible, because they didn't even see me.

A similar thing happened one late afternoon at our new place. Mamma and Aunt Myrtle and Susie were sitting on the back steps and watching the boys playing. Actually I wasn't playing. I was trying desperately to get into the tag game, but I must have been invisible again.

I started crying. Daddy said, "What's wrong?'

I said, "I wanted to play too."

"I didn't know that."

I didn't often sass Daddy, but I said, almost yelled, "Why did you think I was out there running around in circles like Ol' Rattler havin' a dog fit?"

Actually Ott and I were usually trying to outdo each other in the comedy division. One day when kinfolks from town were visiting, Ott and I were in the barn loft, and several people were in front of the barn. Ott took the opportunity to perform a comedy routine making faces, as he stuck his head out between the logs in the wall of the barn. The logs had never been chinked, in order to let in plenty of air to keep the hay dry, that was stored there.

All of a sudden the impromptu audience saw him looking out between the logs. He got a big laugh. I thought I could do the same thing and maybe sing a song or something to top his performance.

I got my head stuck through, but it was painfully obvious that I wasn't going to be able to back out as easily as Ott had done. I did get a laugh, but not the laugh I was expecting and hoping for. It was a real dilemma. When the men came up to the loft to examine the situation there was a consensus that they would have to jack up the roof of the barn for me to extricate my head. I was determined that was not going to happen. So with great effort and lots of scratches and cuts on my ears, I escaped.

Ott said, "Your big ears."

I said. "Well it was easy for a pinhead."

At the dinner table, Ott and I would carry on some kind of banter. Of course, he wouldn't laugh at any of my jokes and I reciprocated with a stony face, while others were breaking up with laughter.

The kinfolks liked to come on Sunday about the time we'd be finishing up after church with Sunday dinner. I figured they would time it like that because they knew that Mamma would have cooked a nice cake or pie. Whatever it was it would be topped with lots of whipped cream. As we had a cow and got about three gallons of milk every day, there'd be plenty of fresh milk, butter, buttermilk and whipping cream.

One Sunday after dinner, Uncle Burton and Aunt Clarissy were there. Ott and I were doing our usual after dinner show, while everyone was still at the table. Aunt Clarissy had finished her dessert. She was begging me and Ott to quit.

"Reid and Ott, you quit that joking now or I'm

gonna wet my pants." That was all the encouragement we needed. Her response was exactly what she had promised. She upstaged us both.

She had to go get the mop to wipe the linoleum.

The arrival of Mary Evelyn added another interesting element to the Gilbert clan. Susie was 13 and helping with the baby girl, but she was soon making plans for going off to nurses' training. Ott considered Baby Evelyn as knowingly stealing his title of Baby Ott.

Actually the aunts and uncles continued to call him "Baby Ott" till he was grown and occasionally after that. They had remembered how he, even as a three-year-old, had flummoxed them.

We were on our way back from Virginia when we took a potty break. In those days there were no service stations with public facilities. There were several areas with woods and bushes to accommodate our urgent needs. We each found our private area and returned to the car.

Ott was in front with Mamma and Daddy. Aunt Myrtle, Uncle Jack, Susie and I were in the back seat. We never called them uncle or aunt, because they were like older siblings. Jack was four years older than Susie and Myrtle was two years older than Jack.

After the potty break, they kept teasing Ott, which

they loved to do. Finally one of them said, "Baby Ott you're rotten. You're so rotten you stink."

His quick retort, even while still a toddler, "I do not. I wiped good." That sent them into gales of laughter. But after that they were a little more circumspect how and when they'd tease him.

Not only was I in competition with Ott, but Mary Evelyn was a different kind of competitor, simply by being born; perhaps her birthright.

When she was three, I had to walk to the Tedder's place to milk our cow. The Tedders were away, and their pasture was so much better than ours. Evelyn wanted to go with me to milk the cow. Mama said, "OK but Reid, you make sure she doesn't get stepped on by the cow."

I assured Mamma and we trekked off to the Tedders; Mary Evelyn, Raggedy Ann, the milk bucket and I. When we got there, I had to figure what to do with Evelyn while I milked. There was a shelf about four feet off the ground. I put some hay beneath the shelf and asked her, if she'd like to sit on the shelf with her Raggedy Ann doll. She was a little hesitant, so I said, "You can be my flowerpot." She didn't say anything, so I asked a question, "What does a flowerpot do?"

She thought for a minute and said, "Nothing." I said, "You're right. A flowerpot doesn't do anything but sit still on a shelf and look pretty." The arrangement worked well. I got the milking

---

finished, and she sat still with Raggedy Ann and looked pretty.

When we got back home and Mamma was taking care of the milk, Evelyn said, "Reid let me be his flowerpot."

Mamma said, "What do you mean? How were you a flower pot?"

I explained the whole thing to Mamma and that Evelyn was quite safe sitting on the low shelf and being a flowerpot.

Ott heard the whole discussion. He added his own comment. "She's not a flowerpot. She's a peepot."

"Mamma, Ott called me a peepot. I'm not a peepot. Reid said I was a flowerpot."

Mamma tried to bring an end to the confrontation of her two youngest children. "Ott do you want to apologize to your little sister?"

"Not really!" More caterwauling from the youngest.

Mamma warned him, "Ott!"

"I'm sorry!"

"Mamma does he mean it?"

"Ask him."

"Mamma, he's making faces at me."

Mamma was growing exhausted by the contentious exchange. "Ott, go to your room and close the door."

Everything was peaceful and quiet for about ten minutes, when Evelyn came crying again.

"Mamma, he's still making faces at me."

"Isn't the door closed?"

"Yeah, but I looked through the keyhole and there he was still making faces at me."

They both seemed to enjoy this little game for years.

When Evelyn was seven, one night she woke me in the middle of the night. She was standing in the doorway. When I asked her what was wrong, she simply said, "I'm here. I don't know why I'm here. I'm just here."

Little did she know nor did I realize at the moment that she was reflecting thoughts of many adults not only then but for years to come. "We're here. We don't know why we're here. We're just here."

The Road

The road was Baux Mountain Rd., which extended from just north of Ogburn Station to the Stokes County line (about nine miles). Our place was two miles from the north end, and, in the other direction, two miles from Shiloh Church. The unpaved portion was the four-mile north end. We lived in the middle ... two miles south, two miles north.

Of course, we traveled the two miles south, to church, to school, to town. Although it was unpaved, it was a sand/clay road ... sand spread over it about every six months, on top of the natural clay beneath. It was scraped with an old road scraper, every couple of months.

The road had some fascinating features: the ability to freeze and thaw in winter and the washboard ridges developed across the road.

Let's talk about the ridges. They were caused by cars going too fast. After they would be formed they would fight back, by jolting the very cars that had made them. The bolts on the cars would shake loose, and the cars could be heard, before you even saw them.

When the road workers would venture out our way, they would put up stakes where a paved road should go to straighten the road. A man who lived in Winston but had land across the road from us, would pull up the stakes, thus delaying for several years a new road.

I would walk the two miles to Shiloh Methodist Church, a couple of times a week; Thursday night for choir practice and Friday night for Boy Scout meeting. The two miles to Shiloh, meant two miles back home. When you walk that four miles so often, you learn not to poke along or you'll never get to you appointed destination. Years later, when walking with a girl to the movies, she'd complain that I walked too fast. I had to learn to slow down. Some times I'm told again to "slow down"; certainly not from walking, after my fractured vertebrae, but maybe from my myriad projects.

But back to the scouts: Preacher Reed, who had organized the Scout troop, would sometimes give us a ride home, if it was raining or brrrr super cold. He lived in the opposite direction. He'd say, "Now I hope you boys will help out some young people when you get older, and they need a ride." I've often thought of that over the years when teaching or working with young people.

When I was teaching at Union College, years later, I piled four students in my car and headed to NYC to see real theatre. Somewhere along the way I heard Preacher Reed's admonition, "Some day when you have the chance to work with young people, once in a while give them a ride, when they really need it."

When I became 16 and had my driver's license, I'd drive Ruth Bowen and me in her daddy's old pickup truck to choir practice. The seat was rather slippery; some kind of plastic. The gear shift was on the floor. There were several curves on the road causing anyone in the shotgun position to slide from side to side. Ruth gladly took advantage of that. I gladly took advantage of the gear shift, but that's another story.

The sand clay road, if a little wet, would freeze over in winter. When the school bus would go over them, on the way to school, we could hear the crustiness of the road beneath us. In the afternoon the road would have thawed and could be quite squishy. There were times when the bus would get stuck right in the middle of the road. Then we'd have to wait for someone to come from town to pull us out.

This stuck-in-the-mud event happened only on the way home, never on the way to school, when we could have avoided the "books and the teacher's ugly looks" a little longer.

Actually, I loved school. When I was ten and in the fourth grade, I got the mumps. Of course, I had to miss school. When the bus stopped to pick up Susie and Ott, I cried. I had had perfect attendance for the three and a half years before that. Ott thought I was crazy, to cry over missing school.

Ott didn't go to the same school Susie and I attended. It was a part of the Mineral Springs Consolidated School. The school bus dropped him off at Grasshopper College. It was a four room building, but Miss Crews used only one room to teach the first and second grades. The room had a potbellied stove. The desks were double desks; each holding two students.

Behind the school were two small buildings; the outhouses for the girls and boys. There were two-seaters, just like the desks. The drinking facility was a hand pump attached to a horizontal pipe with eight holes. One of the boys would pump the handle and water would spurt up out of the holes, watering eight thirsty throats simultaneously.

The playground had two seesaws and a pole swing, which was a sturdy steel pole planted vertically in the ground. Attached to the top of the pole were chains which held at the bottom a swing with three small horizontal bars. The swingers would put their arms or legs on the bars, then run clockwise with all of them sharing the same energy. Usually there would be a big girl who would throw her weight around, literally, on the swings. She would set the pace, even as a second grader. But, of course, there were only first and second graders at Grasshopper College.

I can't recall the official name of the school, but the older kids gave the school the name

Grasshopper College, which was about half-way to Mineral Springs Elementary School. When the bus stopped in the afternoon for the first and second graders, one of the older kids, already on the bus said, "Here come the grasshoppers." Someone else added, "This must be Grasshopper College." The name stuck.

If the bus had problems, like getting stuck in the muddy road, the driver, who was a high school boy, would walk to the nearest phone to call the school garage. The nearest phone was usually at the Crowder's.

The power and phone lines ended a mile and a half from us at Al Crowder's, a retired baseball player. He had more money than the rest of the Baux Mountain folks, and probably contributed some cash to a politician for motivation for the power and phone lines to come all the way to his place. Actually, Mr. Crowder was quite generous with the local folks, allowing us to use his phone for emergency issues like medical situations ... also for school bus trouble

It took a few years for us to obtain these amenities of modern 20th century life.

I was in the sixth grade when we got electricity. What a miracle!! All you had to do was pull a string with a little metal tab on the end. The light would come on and fill the whole room. That meant no more Saturday morning chores of cleaning the lamp chimneys.

We always had plenty of newspapers for that. The chimneys of course would get smudged a bit during the week, and newspapers were the best thing to clean them. You simply wadded the paper up and swiped it around inside the glass chimneys. Mr. Patterson, who ran a fish market in town, boarded at Grandma Gilbert's boarding house. He gladly contributed the daily Winston Salem Journal for us to clean the lamp chimneys. He collected papers from others for wrapping his fish, but he liked to encourage Susie and me to "be industrious and useful", as he called it.

We also got a GM Fridgidaire for keeping milk and other stuff from spoiling. I didn't need to put the milk jugs in the cool box at the spring.

Daddy liked to go frog gigging at night when he worked on the day shift. One night after bagging about a dozen or so, before killing and cleaning them, he put them in the fridge. The next morning when Mamma opened the fridge to get things for breakfast, the frogs croaked loudly as they jumped out at her. She fainted and revived under the kitchen stove.

Despite that, my little sister Evelyn and I are partial to frog legs. Whenever you're cooking them and put in the frying pan they look like a muscular gymnast's legs ... much smaller of course. When you salt them, they quiver and tremble a bit. However, I've never had frog legs in restaurants that were quite as good as those Mamma would cook.

By this time we had electricity, but the folks never bought a TV until after I had left home. Uncle Burton and Aunt Clarissy had a TV set. I believe her favorite night was Thursday, because of the wrestling.

Although TV was new to me, and I was intrigued by it, I was much more interested in watching Aunt Clarissy. She would yell and cheer—even tell them what to do and demonstrate how to do it ... particularly the hold for her favorite wrestler. She was a show herself.

Uncle Burton was rather stoic. He didn't get worked up that way. He'd watch the wrestlers, of course, then watch his wife, blink occasionally and drag on his cigarette.

————————————)(————————————

Summer Work

Work for real pay involved mostly me, and sometimes Susie and Ott. Of course, it was usually work in the tobacco crop, during the priming (reaping) time when extra hands were needed in addition to the family, even if it would be a large family. When I say hands, I once figured how many times each leaf of the bright-leaf tobacco was handled by hand. The count was 11, which required lots of hands, beginning at priming time.

Two or three leaves that were beginning to yellow (coming in order) were snapped off at the bottom of the stalk. The boys were expected to do this work, and the girls would work at the tobacco barn. The leaves, after being snapped off with the right hand, would be put under the left arm until you had an arm load. Then you'd take your bunch of leaves to a sled, pulled by a patient mule, who did a lot of waiting. When full, the sled would be pulled to the barn which was the designated barn for the next firing.

The primers would have to wear clothing to cover as much of the body as possible, because the tobacco, though green, would leave black tar when it was handled or when brushed by in the field. This was particularly true of any hair on the arms or head, thus long sleeves and hats.

At the barn, the leaves were placed on a table made of boards over sawhorses. Next to the table were the stringers. People sitting on the table or standing would get a "hand" (two or three) of leaves and hand that to the stringer who would have a stick about four feet long, placed in a rack. The stringer would then take the hand of leaves, wrap a string around it and then another hand, flipping it to the other side. This was done until the stick was full and tied off.

That was then placed on a pile of other sticks, prior to taking the sticks into the barn and placed on poles in rows. Each barn could hold between 600 and 800 sticks. After that, the flues below the hanging leaves would be fired for a couple of days until the leaves had been properly cured.

The job of tending to the firings was usually left to the older boys, who would also sleep at the barn, as the heat had to be periodically checked and monitored. That was a good time for inviting the neighbor boys to enjoy their shared shenanigans.

After the firing, the leaves were handled a few more times before being taken to the tobacco warehouses in town for auctioning off to the manufacturers of cigars, cigarettes, chewing tobacco and snuff as well as loose canned tobacco for pipes. My dad used tobacco in all those permutations. At the age of 50, he thought, "How stupid". Then quit cold turkey. He had no sympathy for anyone who couldn't quit using tobacco.

But I digress. The handling of the leaves after the firing, would be done in the fall and early winter, when we would be in school and not needed any way.

I hated that job, but it paid well, a half-dollar a day. The married men, doing the same work as I was, were paid $5, which I thought was unfair. (a clear case of ageism or reverse ageism).

Mrs. Priddy once paid me 13 silver dollars for 26 days of work. I wanted to keep the silver dollars, they were so pretty. Mamma said that I ought to put them in the bank. I was afraid they wouldn't give them back to me. I was right. They gave me paper instead and said that had the same value as the coins. I didn't think so.

Many years later, when in college, I worked again in tobacco in a summer job picking up 1,300 loose Camel Cigarettes every minute, making $1.10 per hour. There was a spittoon at every machine. The women dipped snuff and the men chewed Brown Mule plug chewing tobacco. I didn't imbibe. Smoking wasn't allowed ... for some reason.

One night (I was on the graveyard shift) a fellow

came over to my machine and insisted that I take a corner of his Brown Mule, which I did, reluctantly. I chomped down on it a couple of times, then grimacing I used my spittoon for the first and only time. Bill, the purveyor of the Brown Mule, laughed at my distress. In doing so, he swallowed his Brown Mule. He went home early.

At the end of that summer, Lillian Robertson, an older woman in her 50s, came over to my machine and said, "Reid, you go back to school an' get more book learnin'. I'll be here as long as I can crawl up them steps."

I took Lillian's advice and did go "back to school for more book learnin'" ... to Duke University, which was built by tobacco money.

But I digress.

It was the neighbors who provided the jobs. The farthest up the road was Thelma and Cleve Smith. Cleve was a quiet man, but Thelma was a big flirt. When it was a hot day (every day was a hot day), Thelma would pull up her skirt a bit and wave the hem up and down to cool off. "It surely is a hot day today." This didn't pass unnoticed by me.

Thelma was the daughter of Mr. and Mrs. Gold Tuttle. She and another sister had slipped away from home and married, approved or not by their daddy. She had two sisters who never

---

married, Alma and Gertie (Gertrude). They were wonderful singers, learning all the Grand Ol' Oprey songs while doing the dishes, as they told it. Alma always sang soprano and Gertie alto. I could listen to them for hours.

We were always fed well, particularly the cream corn, at every tobacco job we had. I don't know how all the dinners ... we didn't have lunches ... were so delicious and bountiful. Maybe it was because sometimes the cook would stay at the house, while everyone else trekked off to the tobacco field.

After dinner, we'd have 15-20 minutes to relax while the mules were hitched up to go back out to the tobacco field. The Smiths didn't need to carry their water from a spring. They had a well with a well box placed on a concrete slab. In the few minutes I had at my disposal for relaxation, I stretched out on the cement and had the best 15 minute sleep I had ever had before or since.

What did I need for a conventional bed when the combination of my exhaustion from the morning, a bounteous dinner and a cool surface provided a perfect occasion for sleep?

Al Tuttle lived just north of the Crowder's and about a mile north of the Gold Tuttle family. I believe Gold and Al were cousins. We all knew him as Uncle Al.

He was a regular attendee at Shiloh Church. I

---

have a vivid memory of him and Uncle Billy Bowman, who lived in the opposite direction from Shiloh, plowed up the front yard of the church to sow some grass seed.

They were having a hell of a good time in the church yard, like school boys, although they were both at least in their 60s at that time. They would take turns walking behind the plow in the usual way for plowing, while the other one rode the tongue of the plow, which was quite unusual. But the ground was so hard and stony, it required drastic measures. They figured why not have fun.

Uncle Al drove a Model A Ford. He drove so slowly that he was a menace on the roads. In fact, he once pulled out of a secondary road so slowly that a truck turned over trying to miss him.

The older boys liked to tease him and his automobile. One Sunday, after he went into the church building, the boys picked up the rear end of his car and put a block of wood under each end of the back axle ... just enough to get the wheels off the ground.

When Uncle Al cranked his car and got in to drive home, the car wouldn't move, although the wheels were in gear and turning. He got out to inspect the problem and let out some unchurch words when he discovered what had happened.

Obviously the car hadn't jumped up on the blocks of wood unassisted.

The men, noticing what had happened picked up the back of the car and removed the blocks of wood.

When Uncle Al was driving away, he was still sputtering some rather bad words.

One day when I was working for him, he asked me if I wanted him to tell me about his wedding night. Well, yes, no man had ever told me, a teenage boy, about his wedding night.

"Well, actually, it was the morning after my wedding night. I got up. Marney was still to bed. My overalls were hanging on the bedpost. I picked 'em off and threw them on the bed. She said, 'why'd you do that?' I said, 'Do you wanna wear 'em?' She said, 'No!' I said, 'Well then I'll wear 'em. Just remember I gave you the chance. So then I'll wear 'em'."

It was often a gossip topic around the potbellied stove at Sol James's store, when it was obvious that the wife was bossing her man, and thus "wearing the pants". Uncle Al had given his bride, the chance to "wear the pants".

We also worked for the Spencers. They had no children. Mrs. Spencer told us, while stringing the tobacco, that she had had several miscarriages. I didn't know at first what a miscarriage was. She told us that when she and Mr. Spencer were younger, she'd go running toward him and jump into his loving arms. He was a big man, though his name was Bill Tiny Spencer.

They lived where the power lines had been installed and even had running water. Whenever the colored family would stop by for some water, Mrs. Spencer would let them use the outside spigot. She'd hurry then to get some rubbing alcohol to rub and clean the spigot where their hands had been. She'd tell us about her opinion of the coloreds.

One day I told her about Mamma shopping at Woolworth's. "Mamma heard this black man, who had pinched his hand on something, say, "God," Then he saw Mamma, and finished by saying, "Bless it." Mrs. Spencer said, "But he had it in his heart to take the name of the Lord in vain, so he was just as guilty as if he had blasphemed the Lord right out loud."

She told Susie that it was sinful to "gussie yourself up" by wearing lipstick, bobbing your hair and even using fingernail polish.

Mr. Spencer died and sometime after the funeral, I went with Mamma to visit the grieving widow. She showed us in her bedroom a huge box, where she had Mr. Spencer's best "go to meetin'" clothes (She always called him Mr. Spencer). They were laid out as though he was still wearing them, including a white shirt and tie.

While displaying his garments she said, "Mrs. Gilbert, what will I do if some man comes courtin'?"

Mamma, thinking that would be highly unlikely, said, "Mrs. Spencer, I wouldn't worry about it. "

The next time we saw Mrs. Spencer, she was "all gussied up" with lipstick, bobbed hair and rouge. She had met Mr. Largin at a Primitive Baptist Church. "Mrs. Gilbert, the Good Lord in his mercy has lifted the burden of grief from my broken heart."

She married Mr. Largin, a jeweler in Winston. In due time she left Mr. Largin and moved to Florida with a Pentecostal preacher.

That was the last we heard of Mrs. Spencer. She must have been doing the Lord's work in that wicked state of Florida.

----------------------------------**))((**----------------------------------

The Wards

Between us and the Grays was the Ward family. Lon (Alonzo) and Eva were the head of the household. We probably had more ongoing contact with them than with any other family on Baux Mountain Rd.

The youngest daughter was Imogene. I've written elsewhere how Ruby Gray had tried to teach her and Susie how to dance. That dance class didn't last long. Imogene married a sailor when she was still a teenager.

The youngest son was Junior, about four years older than me. The most impressive thing I recall about Junior was when he had a message from his mother to my mother. I had the mumps at the time. He was so afraid of catching the mumps from me that he wouldn't come in. So he stood at a window and tapped on it. He could talk through the window without opening it.

When Mamma came to the window ... it was right at the foot of my bed. Junior said, "Mrs. Gilbert. Mamma would like for you ..." I didn't hear any more of his message because I fell back under the covers, laughing at him. He was so scared of the mumps that he had to stand at the window in the cold weather to tell Mamma what he'd come to say. He was stuttering so bad that he had a hard time saying anything.

Glenn Ward, several years older than Jr. was rather quiet. He had taken an art course somewhere. I saw an oil painting of a camp tent and fire with woods and stream. I don't know if he ever painted anything else.

Older than Glenn was Marie. Her husband, Joe Griggs, was in the army, so she was living back home with the rest of the family. She had two children, Garland and Linda Kay. One day she came running up to our house, which was about a quarter of a mile from them. She had Linda Kay in her arms. Linda was four at that time.

Marie and Mrs. Ward had been doing the laundry in the yard and were boiling clothes in a big black pot over a fire. Linda was playing close by, and she became interested in the whole washing event. So when no one was looking, she got the spoon in the Red Devil Lye and put a spoonful in her mouth. They saw her, rinsed out her mouth and brought her up for Daddy to take them to the hospital. That was quite a fright. The lye caused her mouth and lips to swell for awhile, but she survived.

It was some time after that that Marie came to our house. Crying, she had a letter in her hand. She showed Daddy the letter from Joe. He was in the hospital and wrote, "I'm missing my left hand." Marie thought that meant that his hand was gone. Daddy said, "Marie maybe it's just injured and he can't use it right now. "

Marie was right. Joe's hand had been shot off. He came home with a claw hook for a replacement of his hand. I was amazed to see how well he could use the substitute hand.

I didn't work for the Wards, but I did hang out with the men at the barn, particularly at curing time, when they would have to stay at the barn to tend the fires. They had plenty of time to visit then. Mr. Ward chewed tobacco, and when I would be occupied with something and looking away. Mr. Ward would yell. "Reid" That startled me, and I looked toward hm. "Catch!" Of course, he and the other men laughed when I caught his tobacco cud.

One of the things I did like about Mr. Ward was he was always whittling. He'd like to whittle walking sticks with lizards, frogs and snakes on them. He would also carve ash trays out of soap-stone which was in one of his fields. I started whittling both soapstone and tree branches. I continue that little pastime to this day.

Years later, I whittled a walking stick for my dad and intended to take it to him when I had booked a ticket on a plane. I couldn't get the cane into my luggage, so I acted as though I needed it for walking. I hobbled up to the waiting area, but there were no empty seats. A little old lady, seeing me struggling with my cane, got up to give me her seat. Fortunately, the boarding process had begun, so neither I nor the kind lady was embarrassed. But I digress.

Back to the Wards. Once when Daddy was at the tobacco barn with me, he noticed that the horses were having some problem. They were stomping the ground, snorting and raring up. They were tied at the edge of the woods. He went to their rescue, and pretty quickly identified the problem. They had stirred up a yellow jackets' nest and were getting stung. As far as the yellow jackets knew or cared, Daddy's legs were just more flesh to fight back from stomping out their home.

They crawled up his overall pant legs and were stinging all the way up. Daddy let go of the horses and ran into the hot barn to shed his overalls and brush off the yellow jackets that were on the inside of the pant legs. He survived, but later he was cautious about potential of nesting places of the stingers.

That same summer the Wards had several disasters; much more serious than yellow jackets. One day Jr. came up to the house and said that they needed Daddy to help them with a horse that had gone berserk. I went with Daddy. The horse was so crazed that he was pushing his head against the barn boards and pushing several of them out. Mr. Ward seemed to know about such things. Apparently the horse had some kind of head trauma and was seeking relief by pushing it against the wall of the barn. They had to put the poor animal down, so they shot him. I didn't stay for the execution.

Speaking of Mr. Ward's knowledge about farm brutes' ailments. We once had a cow that was lying down and wouldn't get up and seemed unable to stand up. Daddy went to get Mr. Ward.

He took a look at the cow, walked around her once, then half way round he stopped. He picked up the tail. About half-way to the end, it fell limp. "What's wrong with the cow, is she's got the hollow tail. So get me some turpentine and a clean white bandage. An old sheet will do, if it's clean."

While Daddy was fetching the medical needs, Mr. Ward took out his whittling knife. He cut a slit in the tail, at the approximate place of the hollow. By that time Daddy had returned with the prescriptions. Mr. Ward poured about a cup of the turpentine into the tail, then wrapped the clean cloth bandage around the tail, tying it with strips of the cloth. We stood there talking and watching Ole Daisy. In about ten minutes, she stood up and started grazing. Daddy thanked Mr. Ward and drove him home. But I digress, again.

Back to the troubles at the Ward's. The same tobacco barn where Daddy had retreated with the yellow jackets, burned down. As the leaves being cured with the heat, get drier, they shrink.

Sometimes they fall out of the string, holding them on the stick. When they fall, they sometimes land on the flue pipe which is hot,

---

supplying heat to the barn. The fallen leaf, being dry, pretty quickly bursts into flame. If the flame is big enough it reaches the lower leaves, four feet from the pipe. Then that priming is burnt up. Unfortunately, the barn, being built of logs, was also burnt to the ground.

Later on when most of their crop of tobacco was in the packhouse, we had a severe thunderstorm. There was a great deal of lightning. Lightning struck a barb wire fence at the Wards. The electrical charge from the lightning ran to a wood post, traveled straight across a dirt driveway to a corner of the packhouse and burned it down. It was a nice nearly-new packhouse. It had 14 barnloads of cured tobacco when it burned.

They lost about 90 percent of their crop that year. It's hard to imagine how many hours of work were destroyed.

One may wonder how we knew how the lightning traveled that path I described. There was no way to determine where the lightning struck the barb wire, but the post had a groove cut out all the way to the ground. At that point a furrow was cut across the lane. The furrow ended at the corner of the packhouse.

Mr. Ward liked to go to Sol James's store at Flynt's Crossroads. The store had a pool table, a few groceries, a pot-bellied stove and beer. While the younger fellows would play pool, the old fellows would sit around the potbellied stove and talk; telling old tales, gossiping and joking.

Across the road from the Sol James establishment was the Pentecostal church where Preacher Hutchens preached. Sol's customers, just by being there, gave the Preacher something to preach about.

Sometime after the Ward's disastrous summer, school had started. When the school bus stopped at the Priddy road, the bus door was opened to let off Orene, Lloyd and Junior. We saw Mr. Ward's truck. It was off the road, turned over, but headed toward home.

That was the last I saw of Mr. Ward. He was headed home.

————————————)((————————————

Choices in Life

The Taylors lived on the other side of the spring from us. Mrs. Taylor's given name was Elizabeth. So Elizabeth Taylor lived next door to me, but she wasn't Liz. She was about the same age as Mamma.

Mr. Taylor was a bit older than my folks and had been in WWI. He had been gassed in Europe somewhere. I never knew what kind of gas it was, but it caused him to have certain gastric problems. He couldn't drink regular cow's milk. He could have goat's milk and kept a couple of nannies. I tried to milk one of the goats. I certainly knew how to milk, but the nanny's udder and teats were quite different from our cow's. The teats were surprisingly much larger. The skin seemed as fragile as tissue paper. I could get a little milk, but I was so afraid I was going to tear the teat that I quit trying.

There were three Taylor girls when we moved to the farm. Lucille was Susie's age and in her class at school. Peggy was my age and in my class. I believe Helen was a little younger than Ott. Later there were two more children, more girls. When the fifth girl was born at the Taylors, Ott said, "I feel so sorry for Mr. Taylor."

Mamma said, "Why do you feel sorry for Mr. Taylor? I'd think you'd feel sorry for Mrs. Taylor."
"I feel sorry for him, 'cause he doesn't have any

boys to help him with his work. Mrs. Taylor has all those girls to help her."

Mr. Taylor's mother would visit occasionally. Mamma would let us go to the Taylors to play for only an hour at a time. Neither we nor they had a phone, so we might be surprised when we got there. Old Mrs. Taylor was sometimes the surprise. She was 99 years old. Instead of playing with all those girls. I'd sit on their front porch and visit with their grandmother, born before the War Between the States. I was fascinated by her stories.

Across the road from the Taylors, were the Bowens. Although Mr. Jim Bowen owned land there, no house was there until I started high school. Mr. Bowen had been Stokes County Treasurer during the Depression years ... the thirties. At that time the economy was so bad that many farmers lost their farms, because of the taxes. When the land was put on the market for sale, Mr. Jim Bowen had enough money to purchase several farms there as well as farms in the northern edge of Forsyth County where we were living. Actually the Wards were share-croppers and lived on one of the farms owned by Bowen.

As WWII was commencing in Europe, airports in this country were being upgraded. The Smith Reynolds Airport, just north of Winston Salem, was eight miles south of where we were living.

Mr. Bowen owned property, including land and buildings where the airport was expanding.

One of the buildings he owned was a nice bungalow house. Apparently, Mr. Bowen had made some deal with the airport, that he would save them the expense and bother of tearing down the house, he would remove it. That's what he did. The house was moved the eight miles and placed on the farm at the corner of Baux Mountain Road and the Dennis Station Road.

When the house was put there the Bowens were living in Stokes County, and rather than have a sharecropper move into the house, the Bowen family moved from Stokes County to our neighborhood in Forsyth County. We were only two miles from the southern edge of Stokes County.

There were two girls in the Bowen family; Ruth, in my class in school and Eileen, who had recently graduated from Appalachian State Teachers College in Boone, NC. Eileen had been hired by Mineral Springs High School to teach Home Economics. However, she didn't have a driver's license. She had already bought a car, but couldn't drive until she had the driving test and obtained her license. She asked me to drive her to school until she could legally do so her- self. I was delighted to drive her car. That pushed me up a notch or two in the school social ladder to be able to drive to school and be friends with one of the teachers.

Eileen was engaged to Max Gravitt, a farmer in Stokes County. After they married they bought the Spencer farm. Mrs. Spencer, who had been widowed by that time, was a sister of Mrs. Bowen, thus Ruth's and Eileen's aunt. Mrs. Spencer was remarried by then.

Across the Dennis Station Road from the Bowen's were the Tedders. They had electricity, even though they also were beyond the power and phone lines. Mr. Tedder built a transformer, which produced DC electricity. So they not only had electricity in the house, they also had running water. He had installed a pump in their spring house. However, when the war broke out Mr. Tedder got a defense job in Sylacauga, Alabama. So they, Mr. and Mrs. Tedder, their daughter, Eleanor and nephew, Billy Ray Rooks, moved to where his job was.

Mrs. Tedder had an uncle, Mr. Gentry, who moved into their house until they would return after the war. Mr. Gentry asked Mamma if I could help him do some yard work. "I'll pay him of course." She asked me, and I agreed, if I could arrange my schedule around other jobs.

At the agreed-upon time I walked up quite early to be greeted by Mr. Gentry at my new job site. He showed me what he needed. In the first place, he needed to have the lawn mowed. The yard, including front and back, was about 600 square yards. All but a small level spot at the front door, was on a slant.

He didn't have a power mower. It was an old-fashioned push mower, which could clog quite easily especially if the grass was wet, even slightly. I enjoyed having that mower, which was more than I had at home. There I had a pair of Mamma's scissors to trim around the rocks leading to the front porch. At least Mr. Gentry provided a mower in good shape and fortunately sharp. It took all morning and part of the afternoon to finish. My back was really aching. That was when I understood that old expression. "Oh, my aching back." However Mr. Gentry did stay close by, constantly expressing satisfaction with my work. He also provided several work breaks with cold cokes.

He then showed me the second job he needed. At one edge of the yard was a hedge which badly needed trimming. It was obvious that the hedge had not been tended since the Tedders had left the year before. The hedge was 60 feet long, 65 inches high and 30 inches wide.

The tool to be used was a new pair of shears. That afternoon I got about three-fourths of one side finished. That was rather simple, as I could easily reach the sides by standing on the ground. That night I put my math lessons to work. I calculated that each side of the hedge was approximately 300 sq. ft. The hedge also had three angles, which needed to be trimmed. I had reached the first angle that day.

When I got home, Mamma said, "How much did Mr. Gentry pay you?"

"He didn't pay me today. He'll pay when I finish tomorrow."

The next day I returned to my work assignment. Mr. Gentry seemed to be quite pleased to see me. I finished both sides and started on the top, which was an entirely different challenge. I had to stand on a wheelbarrow to reach across the whole width of three feet. I finished mid-afternoon.

Wow. What a job! The toughest, at least the most strenuous I had ever had. Mr. Gentry said, "Reid, how much do I owe you now?"

No one had ever asked me that before. They always told me what they would pay me before the job commenced. I figured up the time, my usual day's wage and the difficulty of the job. I said, "Would $1.75 be okay?"

"That'll be fine." He seemed quite pleased when he looked over the results of my labor, as he dug in his wallet and pocket for a dollar bill and three quarters.

When I got home Mamma said, "How much did he pay you?"

"$1.75."

"Did he offer you that or did you ask that?"

"He asked me how much. I said, '$1.75'."
"You overcharged him. Now you go back and give him fifty cents back. Don't ever overcharge anyone for your work."

I took him two quarters. He thanked me for the money and also for the work.

That became one of my life commandments. "Never overcharge."

Life commandments is an interesting concept. It usually begins while you're still a child, and quite often from something an adult, usually a parent, says.

But it can also be from circumstances. One of my life commandments was "never waste water." That came from my having to tote so much water when I was young.

We had a sharecropper neighbor, Bob Lawrence, who did a lot of work for us when Dad had his arms so full of boils that he couldn't use an axe or a saw. Daddy had so many boils on his right arm that he had to carry it in a sling. He had a couple or so in his left arm. Someone at Hanes, where he worked, had a cure for the boils.

Bob was a hard worker, but a poor manager of his money. When he would sell his tobacco at the end of the year, he'd have the money spent within a couple of months. He had a daughter,

---

Delilah. He loved buying fancy clothes for her, which would cost him a lot of his hard earned money.

From then until the next year's crop was sold, Bob did odd jobs for neighbors. Daddy was happy to pay Bob for his work, because he was such a hard worker. He also was an interesting fellow in a conversation. One evening after a work session, it appeared that a storm was brewing.

It was apparent that Daddy was quite anxious. He said, "Bob, we better get in the house before that storm gets here." We all got in the house. They continued talking about storms. Daddy said, "You need to be real careful with storms. I was once struck by lightning, so I get away as safe as possible when a storm comes up." That was true about his caution. He'd make us kids sit on the davenport, pick our feet off the floor and quit talking. Particularly no laughing. For a long time I thought laughter attracted lightning.

Bob didn't often disagree with Daddy, but he said, "Oh no, Mr. Pete, when you're out on the road walking (he never had a car) an' it's stormin' and lightnin', the light from the bolt of lightnin' lights up the road, an' then you can see for a while even after the lightnin' is gone. No. Mr. Pete, the lightnin' is a gift from God."

I had remembered with horror when Daddy was

---

struck and in a coma for nearly an hour. The
Wards' packhouse being burnt down by a bolt of
lightning was still fresh on my mind. But I
decided then that I could make a choice of my
reaction to lightning. I could choose Daddy's
fear or Bob Lawrence's mantra that lightning
was a gift from the heavens.

Daddy's fear and caution could have been a life
commandment, if I had not met Bob Lawrence. I
continued to use caution in a storm, but I didn't
choose to cringe in fear from it.

We all have life commandments, which we don't
always recognize.

Years later, I was horrified to learn of a life
commandment I gave to my daughter Tari. Once
when I was discussing the concept, she said that
I had convinced her she was going to hell. I
knew she listened carefully to my sermons.

I said, "Why would you think such a thing? I
never preached hellfire and damnation."

"Don't you remember your favorite saying?"

"I suppose not. What was it?"
"Whenever I said that I had meant to do something, you said, 'The road to hell is paved with
good intentions.' I had some good intentions
and even some bad ones. So no matter what my
intentions were, I was going to hell."

A word of caution to clueless parents and other naive adults. Be careful what you tell a child, even in jest. It could become a baseless, even harmful, life commandment.

Life commandments come with a cost.
Without them one would be lost.

————————————)((————————————

Other Neighbors Other Jobs

The best summer job I ever had was in 1945, just before my 15th birthday and the winding down of the war with Japan. The war with Germany had just ended. I had missed the draft by a few years. All four of Mamma's brothers were serving in some military unit, somewhere on the globe.

The job that summer provided lots of exercise, camaraderie with roustabouts, driving a farm truck and working with sturdy draft horses. We also had scrumptious farm-fresh dinners, maternally cooked by Mrs. Knight.

My fellow workers were Buck and Charlie. They were even more hillbilly than me.

But I had a great deal of respect for them and even for the word HILLBILLY, although some folks used the word as a put down. I had learned at Methodist Youth Fellowship meeting that "Billy" in Australia meant "Friend". Thus HILLBILLY meant MOUNTAIN FRIEND.

I worked all summer barefoot at Mr. Knight's sawmill. Buck, only a few years older than me, said, "Reid, you gonna get them toes smashed, if you plan to go all summer without boots. Or any kinda shoes."

Charlie, several years older, said, "You know you'll hafta snake some logs with Kate, an' she's allus rarin' to go."

"Well, we'll see. I've snaked logs before."

Buck, chimed back in, "Why I've seen a log jump three feet in the air when it hit a little stub an' Kate was pullin'."

Charlie again, "An' you know when Kate goes 'round a stump or tree thet log can roll."

Buck back in the game of intimidation. "It'll roll all ovah you, if you ain't quick with yoah barefoot jumpin'."

"I reckon I can jump quicker an' higher barefoot than with a pair of heavy brogans ... But we'll see."

"Yeah, we'll see all right." As they both laughed at this stupid, skinny kid. They both felt superior to me, even though they both were aware of my interest in education and my plan for going to college. Charlie couldn't even read. But in that situation they were both superior to me. I knew it and acted accordingly.

Room and board were provided for the sawmill hands, but I stayed at home, only about half a mile up the Dennis Station Rd. The board of course was equal for all of us, including Buck and

Charlie. But there was a room, actually the tack room, where the harnesses, saddles and other horse stuff was kept. They had cots for sleeping. The bathroom facilities included an outhouse, washpans on a shelf on the back porch and the creek for their weekly baths.

At the beginning of summer, Ruth, 15, the Knight daughter, wanted me to help her build a bridge across a ravine down in the pasture. Actually, Mr. Knight had already had Buck and Charlie span the gully with two logs, maybe 15 feet long, and about four feet apart. They had also used scrap lumber to build a floor for the bridge. But that was it ... no hand rail.

Peck, Ruth's nickname, had fixed a little picnic on the far side of the bridge. Otherwise the bridge didn't go anywhere. She wanted a hand rail with pretty supports from the logs. So we spent two days gathering mountain laurel branches, bent in several ways for visually interesting bridge siderails.

After two days of wasted labor, as far as Mr. Knight could figure it ... a full dollar for my time at 50 cents a day. I was needed for heftier jobs.

Before the saw could do its job, the logs had to be brought to the mill. So off to the woods where the trees had already been felled. I rode in the log truck with Charlie, driving. Mr. Knight and Buck were in the pick-up. On the way out to the woods, Charlie gave me some lessons in driving. I suppose you might as well start with a heavy truck as with a smaller vehicle.

The horses were already at the logging site, where Buck and Charlie had brought them the day before, while Peck and I were working on her bridge. They were huge horses. Of course they were the size you'd need to pull those big logs, 20 feet long and some times 24 inches thick.

"You still gonna work barefoot like that?" It was Buck, still joshin' me about no shoes, sayin' also, "Sorry yoah fambly is so poah, they can't buy you no shoes." Actually Daddy worked in town at Hanes hosiery and made much better wages than these loggers.

Buck and I would take turns at snaking the logs. I would take a log up to the truck, where Charlie and Mr. Knight and Ol' Pete, a mule, were to load that log. After Buck snaked the first log, he helped me hook up my log. The fellows had been right about the strength and speed of Kate. She did hit a little snag with the butt of the log. It did, indeed, jump off the ground at least two feet.

When we made a sharp turn, the log chain had a swivel link that allowed the log to roll freely. On that issue, I was right, because I found it rather easy to jump across the rolling log, even though we were moving quite fast. If the chain didn't have a swivel link the chain would knot up, causing problems at the end of the run. After that first run, we were supposed to take turns, but Buck kept complaining of his bum knee.

He started congratulating me on being so strong. He was also quite impressed about my jumpin' barefoot over the log. "I nevah seen no body jump across a rollin' log like you, an goin' so fast too. I surely weren't as good as thet when I was 14 ". He knew I'd take the hint and volunteer to take extra trips with Kate. I believe that I took two to three trips for each one of his.

The next day, at the sawmill itself, I had to keep the logs straight and parallel with the carriage, which carried the logs to the saw. It was also my job to get the next log in place for sawing. Mr. Knight controlled the front end of the log, the front dog, the speed of the carriage and the gauge determining the width of the board being sawn. Everything is probably understood, except the dogs. They were the metal spikes to hold the log in place for sawing.

Charlie had to keep the motor running and Buck's job was to work on the stack of logs, keeping them rolling to me for the mill. I kept noticing Charlie occasionally signaling Buck to look at me to see if my toes were smashed yet. It was an apt activity, as there would be times when I would be turned away from the logs rolling down for my attention. Neither one of

the other men would deliberately endanger me,
but they both wanted to see the scene when I
would lose the bet about my toes. If a mishap
would have occurred they would have laughed
for a couple of minutes, then rushed to do whatever they could to relieve my agony and distress.
I even cheated them out of that opportunity.

That was generally the pattern of the summer ...
until August 15, 1945.

We broke work for lunch at the usual time.
Charlie ran to the mailbox to get the paper,
which was always the previous days. He couldn't
read, but I was teaching him to read the
headlines. We had heard on the radio the night
before that Japan had been bombed.

We farmhands were doing our usual
preparations for dinner; putting the horses away
and fed, getting more water for the kitchen,
washing hands and faces. Mr. Knight made sure
we came to Mrs. Knight's table, so he watched
as we wet our hair and combed it down.
Charlie's hair prep was somewhat easier,
because he was mostly bald with just a fringe
from ear to ear.

Charlie was first to primp himself, as he was
anxious to get to the news in the paper. He sat
in a chair just inside the kitchen door, unfolded
the paper with the headlines prominently
displayed. He started reading aloud to impress

us all with his new reading ability. Slowly "THE ... WAR, what's that word, Reid?" "With" "WITH ... that next word?" "Japan" "Oh yeah JAY PAN."

Mr. Knight interrupted the performance by telling us all to sit down, but not before Charlie said, "Ain't it a blessing now that that ol' war is endin'?"

I could see that Mr. Knight was trying to keep anyone from talking about the war, particularly it seemed about the end of the war. He had noticed that when talk started about the end of the war, Mrs. Knight grabbed her heart, as though she had been shot.

I knew she had a cousin or some kin folk killed in the war, and as long as the war was raging, the boy's death and life stood for something. She was afraid that when the war ended, it would be only in history books to be quizzed on school tests.

After the big news of the war ending, the summer kind of wound down before school would be starting. Mrs. Knight baked a special cake for me, to be shared of course with the other men.

Charlie said, "I had you figured all wrong, 'cause you like books an' school so much. But you done a decent job this summer."

Buck piped up with a big mouthful of pound cake, "An' barefoot. You know we had a bet this summer 'bout thet?"

"What was the bet about?"
Charlie said, "It was about the date you'd get yoah toes smashed. The one who'd pick the closest day, would get the jackpot."

"Which was how much?"

Buck said, "It was 50 cents apiece each day until it happened. Now as, yoah toes didn't get mashed, yoah toes won."

"Whatta you mean?"

"An' since it didn't happen, it's our offerin' for you to put away to go to college."

"Now I can't accept that from you guys."

Charlie again, "We won't miss it, 'cause we was gonna lose it anyways."

Buck said, "An' it kinda pays you fer learnin' me to start readin.'"

> '45 was important for our nation
> That summer I took no vacation
> I'd have to say
> That in a strange way
> My toes contributed to my education.

Fried *Dried* Apple Pies

On the Baux Mountain farm someone had years earlier planted several fruit trees. In the front yard were four plum trees, two of which had large sweeter plums. We usually just ate the plums right off the trees, which were easy to climb. Mamma did make plum jelly and occasionally plum pudding with the plums.

On each side of the house were huge cherry trees; one on each side. Their trunks were almost four feet in diameter. The cherries were also eaten in the trees. Mamma was quite concerned about us climbing those trees which reached higher than the two-story house. At the edge of the woods there was a much smaller tree which had exceedingly sweet black heart cherries. Daddy used the assorted cherries to make some pretty good wine. At least we kids overheard the men at the corn shuckings congratulate Daddy on the quality of his brewing.

The apple trees were the most plentiful, as well as the most useful. There were two apple trees in the sweet potato patch, one between the house and spring and two more in the cornfield toward the dark woods. Johnny Appleseed must have stopped by years earlier.

The trees bore a variety of apple types. Before they were even ripe Mamma would use them for apple pies. She said they were better to use in pies that way. Of course we would also start eating them raw, before they were completely ripe. Mamma warned us about green apples causing belly aches, to no avail. We survived.

The real apple treats were fried apple pies They were also the most labor-intensive. As the apples would begin to ripen. Mamma would tell us kids to start the harvesting.

We had already picked blackberries for jams and jellies. The huckleberries would've been ripe at the same time, but they were too small for adequate amounts for canning. Dewberries, which were on vines close to the ground were quite sweet, but only a few. We'd put them in with the blackberries ... the ones of course which we didn't eat.

We would pick apples off the trees or pick up the fallen ones until we'd have about two pecks (half a bushel). We'd lug those to the house where Susie and Mama would peel and core them. Then they'd be cut into thin slices.

While that process was being conducted, I would get a clean white sheet and take it to the barn. I'd put a ladder up against the barn shed which had a metal roof and a only a slight incline. The sheet would be laid out and a rock put down on each corner ... to keep the wind from blowing it away.

By the time this task was accomplished, the apple peelers would have prepared enough of the apples to begin the next step. I would take the slices and put them in rows on the sheet. By the time we had finished the procedures (peeling, coring, slicing, putting them on the bed sheet) the slices would have filled the sheet. At the end of the day, I'd have to get the apple slices and wrap the bed sheet around them to be brought into the kitchen.

The next day, I'd have to put the sheet out again, placing the slices into rows again. At about noon I'd climb back up and turn each slice over, so that side would begin to dry out and brown like the other side (that was solar power). At the end of the day, I'd have to collect them and bring them back into the kitchen. There'd be one more day, repeating the first two days.

This whole process would be repeated a few days later with a new batch of a half bushel of apples. By the time the daily process and the repetitions were finished it would have accounted for about five bushels of apples. This meant fifteen days of drying apples.

As fall weather was beginning to blow, we'd pick a sunny day and put all the apple slices out for one final day of drying. All of the five bushels would have shrunk to about a peck (¼ of a bushel). That would be sufficient for about twenty days of the finished (cooked) product. Mamma would hang the bag of dried apples in a corner behind the cook stove. It would be dry there, as well as a place where she could monitor any predators, like impatient kids.

We could hardly wait for cold weather when it would be timely for fried apple pies. The whole summer process of preparing for the treats several weeks later, gave us a lesson in planning, processing and waiting. We did eat fresh apples in the summer, but there was no instant gratification of fried apple pies. Our tasty reward was at least a couple of months away.

One cold morning I noticed that Mamma left the large frying pan on the top of the stove, after cooking our eggs. I also watched her set the cinnamon on the cabinet counter. I had watched Mamma cook the pies so many times that I was sure I could do it myself.

The first thing to do was to make the dough, which I couldn't do. Then it's rolled out quite thin. In the meantime, the cook has taken about the right amount of the dried apple slices for a dozen pies. The apples would be cooked and smashed into a puree consistency. A dollop of the cooked apples would then be placed on the dough, which is folded over the dollop. The cook would then take a round plate and roll it around the lump, thus cutting a half-moon shape. The cut edges are then crimped together with fork tines.

The frying pan is already hot with a tablespoon of lard and a tablespoon of butter. The half-moon pie is put into the pan to fry each side until golden brown. Several could be fried at the same time. After they're cooked, they're put into the warming oven until they're served.

We could usually smell them by the time we'd got off the bus.

This particular day was somehow different.

We went running to find Mamma in the kitchen.

I was the most persistent. "Mamma, where are the fried apple pies?"

"What makes you think that I would have fried apple pies today?"

Susie said, "The way you placed the fry pan this morning."

Ott said, "Wasn't that why you got the spices out this morning?"

"I didn't say anything about fried apple pies this morning, did I?"

I added, "But as this was a really cold ..."

She didn't give me a chance to finish. "You're all entirely right. but something has happened to

the apples."
Ott asked, "Happened? Did somebody steal our apples?"

"No! Nothing like that. And after you all did so much work, gathering ..."

This time I didn't let her finish. "But what terrible thing could've happened?"

"After I started making the dough, I took down the sack of apples, and when I opened them I found that they were full of bugs and worms ... Sorry ... I had to throw them out to the chickens."

Missing the first day of fried dried apple pies was bad enough, but for the whole winter we would be deprived of any of this much-anticipated cold weather treat.

Three disappointed kids! But another life lesson ... This time of wins and losses. Earlier family losses like becoming nearly homeless, had been shielded by Mamma and Daddy.

This loss belonged to us. Our summer investment of time and effort had bottomed out.

——————————————————————)((——————————————————————

Me and Mrs. Garner

"Mamma, here comes Mrs. Garner."

"Well help her up the front steps, like always."

"Yes, Ma'am."

Only four steps for the five-year-old to maneuver
and assist the old woman, who had come
to visit her neighbor again. She always
attempted to make her visits appear like just
another friendly neighborly visit, but there was
always a purpose to serve some real need in her
lonely world.

Mrs. Olive Garner dressed like one of the witches
in the boy's borrowed reading books. She wore
all black, including her bonnet. Her long black
dress covered the tops of her shoes, which were
old-fashioned hook and eye laced up high-top
shoes. She also carried a black parasol, rain or
shine. It was a bit frayed ... not completely
keeping the rainwater from her thin shoulders
nor the sunlight from her weathered face.

Her clothing as well as her personal appearance,
perfectly matched her spooky wisteria-covered
house. It even seemed that cobwebs from the
house were permanently etched onto the old
woman's face. In front of the house was the new
paved road, only a few feet away from the front

door. Behind was the old sand-clay road, only a
few feet away from the former front door. Each
road curved a little to accommodate the old
house, thus forming a narrow elongated island.
Her house and dilapidated barn were enclosed by
a high chain-link fence, which kept her ferocious
German shepherd dog, named Wolf, away from
people.

There was never any report that the dog had ever
harmed anyone. The fence and the heavy
chain on the clothesline prevented any contact
with the outside world ... However, any time
anyone would walk down the road past Mrs.
Garner's place, that dog would bark and growl
fiercely, all the while straining at his chain to get
at the intruder,whoever or whatever it might be.
The boy had been frightened half-to-death many
times by Wolf clamoring for a dinner of freshly-
killed succulent meat.

People said that Mrs. Garner had a cat, but the
boy had never seen one, whenever he would walk
by there. Apparently the female cat was kept in
the basement to keep it from running away.
Occasionally it would escape for a few days. Mrs.
Garner was afraid that it might stay away like Mr.
Garner, so she'd look for the cat, Molly, up and
down each road, calling "Molly, Molly, come to
Mamma, Baby." She usually could find the cat by
sharing some of her own fish lunch.

Molly couldn't be chained up like Wolf, but was

imprisoned in the dank, dark basement. Even though adult cats did quite well in chasing their prey in the nighttime, without any light the off-spring would have problems; their eyes would not always develop fully.

Mrs. Garner neither saw nor heard very well. She lived alone, although not widowed ... not even a grass widow. However, the boy soon learned that there was a Mr. Garner, who was a couple hundred miles away, near the coast. Mr. Garner, whom the boy had never met, would write occasionally, whenever he needed some extra cash for his enterprise in eastern Carolina. According to some old-timers, Mr. Garner had some kind of "monkey business", which befuddled the boy.

Whenever the mailman would have left a letter for Mrs. Garner, she would hastily head to the boy's mother to read the correspondence from Mr. Garner. The mail would always, or nearly always, be from Mr. Garner. The old lady was illiterate and needed assistance in reading the letters as well as writing letters to her "Dearest Darling", away on a business trip. How long he had been away was anybody's guess. And what business he pursued so far away. was also unknown, despite the nosy neighbors' conjectures.

Mrs. Garner never spoke to the boy, even when he helped her up or down the steps. But, while looking into his eyes, she would give him a big smile, whenever he assisted her. He wondered if she might be thinking of her son. It was never clear about her son; whether he had been killed in the war or had run away from home, years ago. The boy suspected that she had never borne a child, except in her mind and heart. Whatever her past or their current non-verbal communication, there was an immutable silent bond between the two of them ... the young boy and the elderly neighbor lady.

The boy had overheard the old men at Mickey's store, talking about the Garner place of the past. One of them was old enough to remember some of the actual goings-on, particularly the gatherings of the young folks. It was told that when Olive Goins was a petite young woman, she was courted by several hopeful swains, but her attention seemed to be focused mostly on Tom Garner.

However, that was before a city slicker from town started attending the frolics held frequently in the threshing room in the Garner farm barn. It must be said that the parties weren't as splendiferous as the cotillions on the cotton plantations, closer to the coast. The Garner parties tended to be rougher around the edges, both in manner and deed.

The fellow from town was a handsome chap, riding in a fancy buggy (actually a surrey), pulled by a prancing bay Morgan horse. He obliged the girls with rides in his surrey, which had ornate nickel-plated hardware and rubber tires. Of course, there was only room for two in the riding vehicle, which meant he had time to chat with each of his passengers, and they had the same opportunity with him.

This arrangement also included Olive, who was much taken with the young man.

As the town visitor's attendance increased, so did the contentious atmosphere of the Saturday night gatherings. He had begun bringing his guitar and would join the other musicians for part of the evening. The last time he showed up, he played his guitar only for a short while, before he joined the dancers. He began limiting his dance partners to Olive Goins.

Rather quickly, Tom Garner invited him to step outside. Then after about half an hour, the outlander, nose bleeding, rushed to fetch his jacket and guitar. He just as frantically left, bleeding profusely on his expensive guitar and new coat. Everyone could hear the horse, surrey and guitarist, hurrying back to town.

Tom rejoined the party. His clothes were mussed up a bit, including a knife slash across the front of his shirt; but no blood. The other suitor never attended any other frolics. It appeared that Tom had won the hand (and heart) of Olive Goins and brought her home with him to the Garner farm.

So far as the boy's contemporaries knew, the couple had no children, even though Mrs. Garner would mention from time to time a son named Billy. When asked if that was a nickname for William, she'd quickly change the subject.

The Garner farm prospered for several years, but as the markets changed, the Garners were forced to sell bits and pieces of the farm for homes for workers at the new factories in town. No one was riding surreys or buggies any longer. Mr. Henry Ford had changed transportation forever. So people, who had moved from the mountains for factory jobs, didn't have to live in town. With enough land for a house, a garden, some chickens and maybe even a cow; the new folks hoped some of their former lives could continue.

The Garners took advantage of the population shift, selling portions of the home place, until their debts caught up with them again. Mr. Garner, a garrulous fellow, proved to be a better salesman than a farmer. Thus he became a Singer sewing machine salesman. This, of course, took him away from home quite often, the head-quarters and distribution center, being several miles to the east. This required increasingly longer excursions from home. By the time the boy had met Mrs. Garner, Mr. Garner had not been home in years.

On this particular visit, Mrs. Garner's mission was

to have the boy's mother read the letter from Mr. Garner and write a reply from his wife. His letter started off , "Dear Olive, The business here is doing well, but I need a bit more cash for personal expenses." The letter went on for a few more sentences, ending with "maybe sell off an acre or two. Your Beloved Husband, Mr. Tom Garner." He kept his letters, even to his wife, on a business, rather formal, level.

The old lady started dictating a letter, immediately after the boy's mom found a pen and paper, "My Dearest Darling, How wonderful to hear from you. It's so lonely here alone without you. It's not that I'm scared. Wolf sees to that. He won't let anyone through the gates. Though he was only a puppy, when you left on your business trip, he's a very big dog now. The house needs some work, 'specially some painting. I can't do that work any more, and besides paint costs money, which I don't have. You know I would do my best to follow your wishes about selling some more land. I'm sorry to the house stands. I forgot to say that the front porch has pulled away from the house. But the planking on the porch is okay to walk on. I can walk on the safe spots. No one else is walking on it any ways."

The boy's mother urged him to go outside and play, so he didn't hear any more right then. He played awhile by himself, but there was no one else to play with, so he came back just in time to hear the end of Mrs. Garner's letter to Mr. Garner. "I'm counting the days 'till I see you again. Your loving wife, Olive." The boy wondered how many days the lonely old woman had already counted ... waiting for "Dearest Darling" to return.

He was anxious to hear what more the two lady neighbors might talk about. Mrs. Garner had brought a fabric bag stuffed with some of her sewing. Mr. Garner had given her a treadle Singer sewing machine, before he left on his business trip, so she didn't need to hand stitch all her sewing. She retrieved from her carpet bag several cloth wall hangings that looked like cats. At least the top of them had an embroidered cat face with real whiskers, which she had probably combed from Wolf. The bottom of the hanging was a pocket for holding women's stockings, that needed laundering. The fabric of the hangers was bed ticking, showing age and prior use. However it was beautifully hand-stitched. It was probably cut from the bed ticking of an old mattress from one of the many bedrooms. In the younger days of the old house many guests, at times errant travelers, would fill the rooms to capacity.

However by the time the boy's family lived in the neighborhood, the Garner house's rooms and beds were devoid of additional sleepers.

Mrs. Garner was successful in selling two of the cat wall hangings to the boy's mother. When pressured to buy at least a couple more, the younger woman said, "Mrs. Garner, I had already bought two of your beautiful stocking holders, now four in all; one for myself, and one for my mother. Now I'll give these two as Christmas presents to my sisters in town."

Mrs. Garner was desperate for a larger sales day. "Could you take them to church and sell them to ladies there? They'll need Christmas presents too."

"Now Mrs. Garner." The boy could see that his mother was getting really upset, but he knew that his Mom felt sorry for the elderly neighbor. "Mrs. Garner, I don't sell things at church. I go to worship." It had been a long time since Mrs. Garner had attended church, but she understood that she had reached the bottom line of her good neighbor's tolerance, who was more than a little irritated. Mrs. Garner didn't soften her assertive sales push, but she did change her line of merchandise.

What surprised the boy the most, after the hanging cats, were her last items she offered for sale. She slowly and deliberately, began to un- lace her right shoe. She didn't seem to be in a hurry to unshuck her foot from the shoe, even though she was quite efficient in the complicated task. It was fascinating to watch, as she used a hook in the unlacing. They were the old- fashioned hook and eye shoes that fashionable ladies, a long time earlier, wore for special occasions. They extended well above the ankle and were called "hook and eye", because they required a hook to lace up the 12 eyes and 20 button hooks on each shoe.

As she was taking off her shoe, she was staring out the window with no eye contact with either the boy or his mom. Even when the unhooking and successful removal were accomplished, she still sat there almost transfixed in a dreamlike state. It was quite awkward for a minute or two. She was no doubt dreaming of earlier days when she, Olive Goins, was indeed the "Belle of the Ball", wearing those shoes or earlier versions of them.

She then recovered her composure enough to pursue the culmination of her mission. She said that if she sold her shoes, she might have a few dollars for Dearest Darling. The boy wondered if she had planned to walk home barefooted, if she were successful in this unlikely sale. The look of surprise on the younger woman's face let the older woman know that this was going to be a more difficult chore than selling the wall hangings. The boy couldn't determine whether the expression on his mother's face was a prelude to laughing or to crying over old Mrs. Garner's plight.

His Mom said, Mrs. Garner, I have no need for shoes of that style. No one wears shoes like that any more." Under her breath, the old lady said,

"I do." Then in a more audible tone, "But I don't need these fancy go-to-meeting shoes any more." She no longer went to church or any other social gatherings.

Beginning to move more furtively, she pulled from her carpet bag an old pair of men's work brogans. "These work shoes of Mr. Garner's are what I wear all the time. I can wear only one pair of shoes at a time." She gave a gentle chuckle at her little witticism.

It was obvious that her shoes weren't going to be sold hat day. She rather deftly put her right shoe back on and laced it up, as it seemed an every day occurrence. But even that was a time in her past.

Having completed her spousal correspondence, as well as her sales effort, her mission had been only partially accomplished. She thanked the boy's mother and gave him her normal silent smile. He helped her down the four steps and watched as she walked up the road, still wearing her fancy shoes.

A couple of weeks later, the boy and his Dad walked up the road, past the Garner place to Mickey's store. Wolf failed to greet them as usual. Where was he? Surely he wasn't sleeping on the job. They hadn't seen Mrs. Garner, either. They did see her at the store. As the boy, as usual was intrigued by the old lady, so he was looking at her and not watching where he was walking … until he heard a threatening growl coming from the floor near his feet. Jumping back a couple of steps, while holding onto his Dad, he saw that he had nearly stepped on Wolf. Apparently the guard dog was rather civilized when Mrs. Garner took him out in public. His growl was just a fair warning to anyone getting too close.

Mickey's General Store also served as the local post office, as well as a kind of bank. At least a person could get checks cashed there. Mr. Mickey was helping Mrs. Garner write a check and sending it to Mr. Garner in Everwood, North Carolina. The boy lisened carefully to hear, if she were addressing it to "Dearest Darling". Nope. Just "Mr. Thomas Garner".

Fully aware of the old lady's need for money, the boy wondered how she was managing to send money to her husband. Then he noticed that she was wearing the over-sized men's brogans, even though she was wearing the rest of her social attire with her usual black dress and bonnet and parasol. He reckoned she had successfully sold her fancy shoes, so then she had some money for Mr. Garner's "monkey business".

Not long after that the boy's father lost his job at the mill in the midst of the Depression. As they also lost their new house they had to move again. Somehow Mrs. Garner got word to them that when they left, she would like for them to stop by. She had something "for Billy". Although that wasn't the boy's name, he knew that she had something for him. He couldn't imagine what it might be, as he knew that she had very little herself, and certainly not enough to give away.

After the family's belongings were loaded in the truck, the driver drove to the Garner place and stopped. The boy jumped out of the back of the truck to see what surprise Mrs. Garner had for him. She was standing by the mailbox, holding a paper grocery bag. She gave the boy her usual smile, this time accompanied with words. "Here, Billy, this is for you." While both the boy and the old lady had hold of the bag, he bowed slightly with the only words he ever spoke to her, "Thank you, Ma'am."

It was extremely important to her to be able to share something of and from herself, other than the occasional money to the absent Mr. Garner.

The boy slowly turned and climbed back onto the truck. Anxious to see what Mrs. Garner's gift might be, he quickly opened the top of the bag to find one of her hand-stitched cat wall hangings. He wondered why she had given him this ... maybe to give to his mamma for a birthday present. His wonderment lasted only a few seconds ... expanding to a greater sense of awe, as the cat face wall hanging began to sound like a cat.

In the pouch he felt something soft moving ... quietly mewing. He picked up the fur ball and began stroking the tiny head of a kitten. It was then he noticed that the kitty's eyelids were matted together.

Mrs. Garner had given the boy what she had ... a blind kitten.

—————————————————————XX—————————————————————

Down the Road

Farther down the road from us was Perrell's Springs, which was a mineral spring. It was on private property. As a part of the property there was an infamous dance hall, where there was some kind of Fracas every Saturday night. It didn't really impact the rest of the community much.

Just up from Perrell's Springs was the only colored family: Curtis and Lucy Gray and children. They were some of the best farmers on Baux Mountain Rd. They tended someone else's fields up the road from us. Whenever they would go to those fields, and we were playing ball in the front yard, I'd feel so guilty because they were on their way to work, and I was playing. They'd all be riding on their farm wagon, and wave to us on their way to their work.

Ruby Gray, the youngest of the Gray family tried to teach Susie and Imogene Ward how to dance. I watched, as Ruby got more and more frustrated with her dance students. Finally she said, "You gotta have rhythm to dance. You gotta have rhythm."

That seemed to conclude the dance lessons on Baux Mountain Rd.

One day Ott referred to Mrs. Gray as Mrs. Gray. Mamma said, "Ott, you can't call Lucy Gray, Mrs. Gray."

"Why not, Mamma? She's older than you."
Mamma had a tough time trying to adjust her
children to the norms of segregated Southern
ethics and protocol.

Just across the road from Perrell's Spring was
Camp Civitan, the YMCA camp for colored boys.
It was just fields and woods and a dammed-up
creek for a pond for boating and swimming.
One Sunday afternoon, lots of cars and a couple
of ambulances had sped down the road, rattling
all the way, because of the washboard ridges of
the road. Daddy stopped one of the cars to ask
what was going on. We found out that some boys
had drowned at Camp Civitan. He and I drove
down to see if there was something we might do
to help.

I never had seen the pond before. It wasn't very
large and quite muddy. Curt Gray had been
sitting on a bench watching the boys playing in a
boat. He told us that five boys were in a boat in
the middle of the swimming pond. They became
so raucous that the boat capsized. Even though
none of them could swim, three of them
managed to get to some more shallow water and
wade out.

Two of the boys, young men rather, were still
beneath the water. There was a watergate for
releasing the water, but it was apparent that that
was going to take a lot of time. Dad, who
couldn't swim, said to me, "Son, since you can

---

swim, do you suppose you could go in and get at least one of the boys?" I was only 16, and I agreed to try. I had never done anything like that. Buying some time and maybe a way out of the situation, I said, "Sure, if you can find someone else to help", realizing that there was probably not any of the other men standing around who could swim.

I had learned to swim in Old Field Creek and in town. Actually, I wasn't allowed to swim in the city recreation pools in Winston. Chain link fences enclosed each of the pools for safety reasons. But also to monitor the kids in the swimming classes and free swimming times; the country kids were not allowed in the pool at any time.

However, when I was visiting cousins in town, I would go with them to the pool, and during the swimming lessons, I would stand outside the fence and replicate the movement in the classes. I overheard some parents laughing at this skinny country kid, doing the sidestroke vertical and waterless.

Preacher Hutchens, who was pastor of the Holiness Church at Flynt's Crossroads, said that he could swim. "But I have a palpitating heart and can't go under the water." I wondered what good he could do on top of the water. He had met my excuse for not trying some kind of recovery of dead bodies. He added, "I can hold that float over the spot where Curt said they went down."

We stripped to our skivvies and waded in. I wasn't a very good swimmer. I did go under a few times and touched one of the bodies. I had trouble holding on to the body. The muddy water was not only opaque, but it was also slippery. The water had recently, after a thunderstorm, run off plowed fields into the pond.

What a strange feeling I had: not only the touch, but the inner feelings of trying to find a carcass of a dead man in the murky water. I had never touched a dead person before. I finally found a muscular arm and grabbed it to bring the boy and myself to the top of the water and the float, where Preacher Hutchens was keeping our parking space. I held onto the float and the boy, while kicking my legs to help the preacher get to the shore, which was only a few yards away. It seemed like miles.

As I got to the muddy bank, I handed the young Black man to men standing there. My knees buckled under me, but I didn't fall. It wasn't the weight of the body, although he was quite muscular.

It was the inner weight of my questioning again the racial ethos of the South.

We were told later that Preacher Hutchens had preached long and intense that night ... it was Sunday. He preached that, "When that teenage boy faced death, his knees gave way under him, because he didn't know Jesus, but he did know that one of these days ol' death was comin' for him."

We, white Boy Scouts, did get to use the YMCA indoor pool. Segregation kept us white boys away from the Black boys, and In those days didn't allow the YMCA to include the colored boys. So they got a muddy cow pond.

    Would that the white boy could have swum

    With the Black boy in clear water of life

    Rather than meeting as we did

    In the murky waters of death.

————————————)|(————————————

Gatherings on Baux Mountain Road

There were various gatherings in our neighbor-hood. Of course there were the school gatherings, but they were miles away.

There were happenings at church. Choir practice on Thursday, Scout meetings on Friday and on Sundays, two services; one in the morning and one in the evening.

Choir practice was led by Mrs. Newsome, who was also Susie's piano teacher. Susie had a piano lesson twice a month. I always had to walk with her there. Mrs. Newsome lived on Shallott Mill Rd for a while. Not really near the road but a couple hundred yards off the road. At other times she lived on Red Bank Rd., which was a paved road. In order to make the trek a bit shorter we'd hike through the woods on the Tuttle farm.

I'd need to accompany Susie, because bears might get her, even though we went in daytime. At choir practice, I sang with the baritones. Mr. Colin Weinbarger had built a choir platform to put the choir in view of the preacher and congregation.

Nothing particularly spectacular about choir practice, but when I was 16 I drove the Bowen pickup truck with Ruth Bowen. J. D. Perrell was suspicious of my intentions with Ruth and would sometimes hide in the bushes near the Bowen house to check on any hanky-panky between me and Ruth when we'd drive back from choir practice.

Actually, my girlfriend, Martha Kelly, was also in the choir, but she lived in the opposite direction down Red Bank Road. One evening during choir practice, Martha turned around to look at me, and I was wrinkling my forehead. She said, "What are you doing?"

I said, "Daddy has wrinkles in his forehead, so whenever I'm doing anything serious, I wrinkle my forehead. Then it might come natural after a while."

"How silly."

It was silly, but I wanted to be like my father. The choir, of course, performed for the Sunday morning worship services. For six years, Preacher Ralph Reed was our pastor. He was inspiring to us young folks.

After the worship service we had Sunday School. For a while Mrs. Newsome was my Sunday School teacher. I recall one morning she began talking about the evil of dancing. She was talking like a Baptist, who vehemently opposed dancing. She told of someone she knew who loved to dance, but "Once she found the Lord, she no longer had the desire or interest in dancing."

I said, "Mrs. Newsome, do you wanta know what I think?"

"Yes, Reid. What do you think?"

"I think she got too old to dance and just wasn't interested in dancing any more. Doesn't it say somewhere in the bible that there will be singing and dancing in heaven?"

I knew she would like the singing reference. The class time was over, so the confrontation ended before it even got started.

Later on, Virginia Fulp was our Sunday School teacher. Actually, she wasn't much older than myself, so our views didn't vary very much. Our theological compatibility was also assisted by Virginia's Christmas gift to each of us: chocolate-covered cherries.

On Sunday evening we gathered again rather informally at the church for a kind of singalong. Everyone had an opportunity to suggest a song, and everyone seemed to have a favorite. So you'd raise your hand, and sooner or later they'd get to your request. I had so many favorites in the old Cokesbury Hymnal. I don't know why I've remembered Joe Stoltz's favorite.

Joe was a little older than me, and went to Providence Moravian Church on Sunday morning. I believe his favorite was Ivory Palaces, # 191 in the Cokesbury. Often I've thought of Joe and the first line of the hymn which was "Out of the ivory palace into a world of woe." I haven't known much about ivory palaces, but I have experienced worlds of woe.

Joe was sweet on Marie Scott. She was a pretty thing, and didn't seem to be too interested in Joe, but she may just have been coy. They did later marry. Their son, Benny, married my niece, Mechele.

Joe and Marie are now gone but Mechele and Benny have a family of their own with two sons and I don't know how many grandchildren.

I should say a word about Preacher Ralph Reed. When he came to our church, he was fresh out of seminary and unmarried. He served a charge with three churches. The parsonage was at Mt. Pleasant Church, which was the largest church. All the ladies with marriageable daughters would almost fawn over the wonderful new preacher man we had. Until he married Billie Pennington. They had met in college, before coming to Shiloh. She was from the big city of Charlotte. Some of the church members felt she may have felt bad about serving a country church like Shiloh.

The parsonage wasn't very nice, especially for a young bride. A couple of times I spent the night at the parsonage. The only bathroom was through their bedroom. It was terribly embarrassing going through their bedroom in the middle of the night, when I had to go.

Mrs. Reed had majored in music in college and sang with her book held high in front of her. I suppose she was a diva. The church ladies weren't always nice to Mrs. Reed until their first baby, Mary Elizabeth was born.

One Sunday, Mrs. Reed brought the baby to church. Just as Preacher Reed started his sermon, his baby daughter set up a demonstration of her operatic lung capacity. This continued for about six minutes when Rev. Reed said, "Dear, would you take the baby out?"

As she walked down the aisle, Mrs. Reed was sobbing from the embarrassment of the incident.

After the service was over, all the women rushed to the car where Mrs. Reed was sitting holding the sleeping Mary Elizabeth. The women of the church were commiserating with the preacher's wife. All the men and especially the husbands were under verbal attack by the women. I believe at that moment they would have been candidates for membership in Betty Friedan's Women's Lib movement.

Friday nights we boys gathered for Scout meetings with Mr. Reed as our first scoutmaster. Actually, he organized the troop and had us registered officially as Troop 100 in the Old

---

Hickory Council of the Boy Scouts of America. We thought Troop 100 meant that we were 100 percent; 100 percent of what, we weren't sure. Later, other men provided adult leadership, including Daddy and Ted Bowman.

On camporees with city Scouts, we had an advantage as we already knew about knots, starting fires, cooking over open fires. We didn't know about wearing fancy official uniforms or totin' flags. We learned all that and even how to fold a flag and when and where to display it with due respect at all times.

There were other community gathering occasions such as workings. The working in tobacco was a job and did serve the purpose of easing the work a bit, even as onerous as the work was. Women in the neighborhood would gather, set up a quilting frame on the backs of straight chairs for a quilting bee and share in making quilts. They sometimes had specific patterns like the Texas star. But more often it would be with leftover scraps of fabric, which they would call a crazy quilt.

It would have been impossible for one woman to build the quilt alone. To them this didn't seem like work, and it was a wonderful occasion for getting together and chatting with a lot of gossip, particularly things to be said about the neighbor woman who wasn't there. She would be like the sacrificial lamb to be sacrificed on the altar. Actually, any gossip would be

---

acceptable if it was followed with "Bless her heart."

"Have you noticed that Betsy has gained considerable weight? Bless her heart."

Corn shuckings were other necessary chores which turned out to be gala events with much laughter and horseplay. No one was drinking alcohol openly. The exception would be home-made wine. The farmer whose corn was being shucked could provide a pint or even a quart fruit jar of wine which he or a friend had brewed. That was hidden in the pile of corn to be shucked and whoever found it, could claim it as a prize. By the time he had shared with every-one, there would not be much to take home for future consumption.

Cold weather was hog butchering time. It was another job that needed several hands.

After the gory part of the butchering, the meat carcass would be cut up in several parts. The tenderloin that ran down each side of the backbone was easily cut away. The hams and shoulders would be separated to be smoked, rubbed with salt and spices for curing and hung up or embedded completely in salt to preserve them.

The liver would be removed and cooked, then ground up, adding certain herbs for fried liver pudding. The rest of the meat was divided between lean and fat. The lean would have some fat then put through the sausage grinder. That had to be attached to the edge of a table and hand ground. The meat would be patted into shapes like hamburgers, then cooked and mostly canned.

The fat would be cut into cubes and put into a large pot over an open fire to render lard. The cubes would cook down to small nubbins of meat fiber, which would be skimmed away. The grease left in the pot, would be put into large cans where they would set or gel into a soft solid known as lard.

The nubbins dipped out would be saved and would be cooked in delicious crackling corn-bread.

Another gathering was the chicken stew, which would happen about the time the crops had been laid by (the last plowing) before harvesting had begun. Actually, it was not a stew; it was cream chicken soup cooked in a big iron pot; the one used for boiling clothes and rendering lard.

Everyone had plenty of chickens and milk and butter. Occasionally a freshly-shot squirrel or two might be thrown in. Once when we had the chicken stew at our place, the Starbucks were there.

Mrs. Starbuck had a lot of old time remedies and

superstitions. At one time when I was at their place, Bobby, the youngest Starbuck boy, came running to his mother with a lot of bleeding from his foot where he had impaled it on a big nail at the barn. His Mamma looked at it and yelled for James. "James, go get that nail that Bobby stepped on. Pull it outta the board and bring it here."

James went running for the nail. Then obeying his Mamma he pulled out the nail and brought it to her. She greased the nail, then tied a string to it and hung it up, before pouring turpentine on Bobby's foot and binding it up with a clean white cloth. "That's what you do to keep Bobby from gettin' gangrene." I thought at least the nail will not be stepped on by anyone else ... very practical procedure.

While Daddy was watching the stew boil, Mrs. Starbuck was watching him. They both saw that the stew was about to boil over. As Daddy was stirring the soup, Mrs. Starbuck yelled, "Rub your stomach, Mr. Pete. Rub your stomach."

"Why Mrs. Starbuck?"

"So it don't boil over."

"Aw it won't keep it from boilin' over."

"Now, Mr. Pete, rub your stomach. Do it."
To oblige Mrs. Starbuck, Daddy rubbed his

stomach. The bubbling liquid began to calm down. It didn't boil over.

"Now see, what I told you? It didn't boil over now did it?"

"No, Ma'am, It didn't."

Mrs. Starbuck wasn't the only one with some sense of the supernatural. When Daddy would see someone fixing a roof on a Sunday, he'd say, "It'll leak, if he tries to fix it on Sunday."

There were set feelings about what was allowed on Sundays. One Sunday after getting back home from church, Daddy wanted to check his turtle traps in the creek. He was feeling guilty doing that on a Sunday. Ott went with him. As they were quickly crossing a plowed field on the way to the creek, Daddy heard Ott grunting behind him. He said, "Ott, is there something wrong?" He stopped and looked back at Ott and saw him stretching in the freshly plowed field to reach the indentations of Daddy's footsteps.

Ott said. "It's awful hard following in your foot-steps." That may be a kind of superstition, but also a life lesson which Daddy used the following Sunday in Sunday school.

"Be careful where you're stepping. There may be a child trying to follow you."

A repeated further word of wisdom to anyone watching a pot of chicken stew that's about to boil over the edges of the pot ... so then rub your stomach and you'll have the same success as Daddy, when he listened to Mrs. Starbuck.

Superstitions are used for most holiday occasions. Everyone seems to know that black eye peas are eaten on New Year's Day for good luck. The meat for New Year's is pork rather than chicken, the reason being, the chicken scratches backward for food, but the hog roots forward. On New Year's you want to root forward.

───────────────────X───────────────────

Barnyard Battle

Back home, we raised a few chickens. If a hen found a secret nest and was interested in brooding some little chicks, we left her alone, even if we knew where her nest was. As with all potential mother fowls, she had a rather complicated responsibility. In the first place she had to make sure she had a papa for her off-spring or her eggs would be infertile and not hatch. Usually she would lay about a dozen to a dozen and a half eggs, before she would start setting (brooding).

Every day she would have to reach under her feathers and make sure that each egg would be turned over. Otherwise, the eggs wouldn't hatch. After 21 days the eggshells would start pipping. She must be ready to help remove the shell, if it proved too much for the new-born.

Baby chicks are different from wild birds, which are hatched featherless with bulbous eyes closed and a huge beak, almost constantly gaping open, waiting for food to be dropped in.

The chicks don't need to wait to see. They have their eyes open and have immediate ability to walk and even to scratch for food. Of course, mother hen teaches some of the food-gathering skills to the young toddlers.

In addition to birthing and scratching for food,

---

there were dangers ever present. Mamma hen was instinctually aware of chicken hawks, who were always on the lookout for a luncheon of tender chicken morsels. Whenever the shadow of an airplane would be seen, the hen perceived this as a chicken hawk or falcon. She would quickly call to the chicks, gather them under her feathers and wait for battle.

I never witnessed such a war, but I did see Mamma hen flog some clueless city kid, who tried to kidnap one of her offspring.

Our chickens had another mortal enemy ... a weasel. Weasels, the vampires of the fauna world, wouldn't eat the chickens. They would simply grab them by the neck and suck all their blood.

One spring, my dad decided to buy a hundred day-old chicks (which we called widdies) from the Cox Feed and Seed Store in Winston. We were all set with a brooder with feeding troughs, water containers and a light bulb, substituting for Mamma's warmth.

Being quite aware of the danger of weasels and their ability to squeeze through the tiniest of apertures, we had closed all the holes that would discourage even an earthworm ... we thought. We had covered the flooring with sand, so that the foundling chicks could scratch to their shared delight.

Not good enough! The next morning when we opened the top of the brooder, we were greeted by a horrific sight. A hundred chicks lay sprawled on the sandy floor, their necks having been surgically pierced for the outflow of their life blood.

We didn't buy any more chicks that spring, as the bloodthirsty weasel was still on the prowl. We let Mother Nature take her course, as one of the potential mother hens laid eggs, hatched and brooded the widdies.

She did quite well for several days with her little family of 14 widdies until one morning we saw an awesome, delightful sight. The mother hen and her chicks were scratching for their usual breakfast in the barnyard. Everything was fine, except for the appearance of the mamma ... Her neck was shaved ... all feathers gone.

We realized we had missed a battle royal, some time in the night. The nocturnal weasel had gone hunting, but had not accounted for the ferocity of a mother, even if she were only a chicken.

He had caught her, but had progressed no further than preparing his meal, by clearing the feathery path to the blood-filled artery in her neck. That's as far as he got. She was alive and well, as were her brood.

Not a chicken life lost that night.

---X---

The Farm Brutes

The smallest critters, seldom seen, were doodle-bugs. Now most folks have never heard of a doodlebug, even though they are killers and set their own traps for their victims. A doodlebug is the larva of an ant lion. They hide themselves, so you don't see them without a little bit of coaxing. The doodle could be found in real fine sand. It makes a cone in the sand and then places itself at the bottom of the point of the cone with its mandibles open. When an ant ventures by the top edge of the cone, it slides down into the jaws of the doodlebug for his lunch.

Whenever we'd find a doodlebug trap, we'd get down real close and say real loud, "Doodlebug, Doodlebug come up to see me." We'd repeat that a couple of times, or instead tell him, "Doodle-bug, Doodlebug, your house is on fire." The loud sound would usually arouse him to come out of his hiding place to investigate.

I'm not sure he understood standard American English, but he did understand basic hillbilly.

The larger critters were more like family members than mere brutes. This was especially true of the pets like dogs and cats. However our pets were not house critters.

That was just as well, as they were more free out-side to pursue their own interests. The cats, of course had a great deal more to do outside than if they'd been housebound. That way they were able to catch the vermin before they reached the house.

I should mention some of the vermin. We were successful in hunting down the weasel. His man cave was fairly close to the chickens, but we exterminated him.

We weren't nearly as successful with the rats, until we had a couple of days of rat massacres. When we moved into the old farmhouse, for awhile we kept the chickens in the walk-in basement under the kitchen. We soon discovered that rats inhabited the many holes in the natural earth walls. Daddy hooked a hose to the tail pipe of his car, then inserted the hose into the rat holes.

That took care of the rats for a while in that space. After the barn was built and a crop of corn had been harvested, we noticed once in a while a rat would be seen running under the cornstalks, we'd left after the corn shucking. So the neighbor boys and men were summoned. When they started taking away the cornstalks, rats would run out. They didn't leave en masse. They would leave one or two at a time, giving the armed neighbors a chance to shoot them.

After they were killed, they were simply put in a pile ... 28 of them ... to be disposed of. But that wasn't the end of the story. The carcasses began to disappear one by one. We knew they were dead, but how were they disappearing?

We watched the pile of rats and saw a cat pick up one and head toward the chicken house. She was utilizing the nests as depositories for her cache of rats. She put three rats to a nest, and as it was cold weather, the rats were refrigerated for the cat's daily dinner; one rat a day.

Susie claimed the cats as her pets, and Ott and I claimed the dogs. Susie said that she hadn't seen Lucy for several days. One day when we were in the car ready to go see Kate Hill, Daddy's cousin in Sandy Ridge, Lucy came into the yard, heading to her bed under the porch. Her stomach was cut open and her entrails were dragging on the ground. There was nothing to be done, so we left Lucy under the porch. It was about an hour's drive to Sandy Ridge. That day we had something to talk about, after Susie cried for awhile.

After the weekend at the Hills', Susie didn't see Lucy for two weeks. We figured that the cat had crawled into a warm spot and died. Then she came marching home all healed with a huge scar across her belly. I told Susie, "It looks like she's had an appendix operation."

"Don't make fun of her. She seems to be all healed."

"I'm not making fun of her. I think it's great that she's healed herself. It must have been one of her nine lives."

The cats and dogs got along just fine at our place. They each had their own routines and responsibilities. The dogs of course were meant to be hunters, and that's the way we related to them. When they weren't hunting, they could laze wherever and whenever they chose, and they chose often.

However they were expected to act appropriately for a hound dog. Their tracking with their nose to the ground had to be going in the right direction that the victim was headed. If he was back-tracking, he'd be lying and would get a scolding and maybe a switching.

It was also the responsibility of the hound to know what was appropriate to trail in the daytime (rabbits) and which at night (possum or raccoon).

At night it was a hunter's delight to hear the dog barking with their own individual voice print. Quite often you might hear one of the boys say something like this. "That's Ol' Queenie. Ain't she got a good mouth on her?"

We had a long-legged beagle, named Leagle. Daddy gave him to Gil Easter, but Gil said that Leagle left the second day that he was there. It took him half a day to get back home, which was 10 miles away. We kept him as long as he lived.

There was one fellow, Red Bennett, who traded a lot of hound dogs. There was one dog he couldn't get rid of, because other men knew the dog was a loser. So Red painted the dog with black shoe polish to get rid of him. When it rained the hound's new arrival realized he had been cheated.

Of course you wouldn't want a suck-egg dog, as you lose a lot of eggs that way. One way to cure a suck-egg dog was to bait him with an egg shell in which you would put a lot of hot pepper. It was a sight to see the dance of that dog when you'd see him take the bait.

The larger farm animals required more attention. The cow was Ol' Susie, who's name didn't please sister Sue at all. Sister Susie was constantly being honored by local boys who would often name the newborn stock. I'll call our cow Daisy to avoid further confusion.

Daisy had to be milked twice a day no matter the weather. It was one of my chores from the time we got the cow until I left home, (eight years). Mamma deliberately avoided learning to milk or she would be called on to substitute. She was wise to do so. She had enough to do without electricity or indoor plumbing.

Sometimes in hot weather, Daisy and I both

would be bombarded by horse flies. They were vicious critters, two or three times the size of a house fly. I often wondered why the housefly was given that name, housefly. At least the horsefly would bite horses, as well as cows, but a housefly ... oh never mind.

The horse fly bite was deep and would draw blood. They wouldn't drink all the blood of course, and blood would dribble from the puncture. If I didn't catch them in time there might be as many as a half dozen, oozing blood outlets. They were relatively easy to catch by hand, much easier than a housefly. So I would take my attention away from milking for a moment to catch a horse fly, as soon as he would land on Daisy's side. I'd catch him with one hand, then pull his head off before watching him take his last flight on automatic pilot. He never bit the cow or horse again.

As soon as I brought the milk to the house, Mamma would strain it before saving some of it for cooking. I'd then take the jars of milk to the spring box in the cool water just below the spring. We'd have to put a top on the box to keep the coons from getting the milk, which they'd love to do. Of course later, when we got electricity the milk would go into the Frigidaire.

Still on the subject of flies: houseflies this time. Even though we had screen doors, the flies were at times in swarms. Mamma put up sticky tape to catch some of them. The fly would buzz over

---

to the strip and get stuck. They'd flutter a bit then call it quits. There were still too many to exterminate with a swatter. Mamma would prop something against the screen door to hold it open. Then all of us would get bed sheets (two to a sheet). We'd then flap the sheets toward the door. About 80 percent of the flies got the idea and left the unfriending. The 20 percent left would be attacked with a swatter. In a few days the ritual would need to be repeated.

As another diversion, many years later in college, Bernie Welch, my roommate and another athlete, were competing with each other with a hand clamp to see who could hold a penny in the clamp the longest before the strong spring would spring open. I watched their little game for a while, then said, "Let me try."

They both laughed, because I was a scrawny kid, certainly not a husky muscular athlete. They accommodated my request, handing me the clamp. "Okay, Reid, let's see how you can do." They were amazed when I held the penny in the clamp nearly twice as long as either one of them. "How did you do that?"

"When you've been milking a cow twice a day since fourth grade, your hands get plenty of exercise to develop a lot of strength ... if not brawn."

But I digress in relating the extracurricular activities of Daisy. She and maybe the horse would get out of the pasture field, into the corn field and eat the green corn stalks. Whenever that would happen they would eat so much that they'd founder themselves. Founder is a strange word, because it can have exactly opposite meanings. To be the founder of an organization is to start it. However if it founders, it fails. It is a different word than flounder, which is a fish. If something flops around it flounders, not founders. I say all this to have the reader know what the farmer already knows that for an animal to founder himself, he has eaten too much. That could be fatal.

So when Daisy would founder herself, she'd need a dose of Epsom salt. In order for the Epsom salt in water to be taken by the cow, they'd need to lash a rope around her horns to hold her head up, so that when the quart of liquid would be poured into her mouth she would naturally swallow it. This treatment meant that the stomach gas would be released, thus saving the dumb brute. We would give that treatment in the front yard where there was a substantial tree branch to hold the critter's head up. I'm sure anyone passing by thought we were executing the poor animal on a hangman's noose.

A horse would get a similar treatment if he ate too much green corn. An interesting little-known factoid is this; a mule would never founder himself. If he got into the green corn he would eat enough, but not eat too much to founder himself.

A mule is a hybrid, the offspring of a jackass and

a mare. Pound for pound the mule was much stronger than a horse. The mule also had smaller hooves and therefore much more surefooted to take tourists into dangerous places like the Grand Canyon. As they are hybrids they are asexual, or unisexual, but some would be given a male name and some a female.

We had a mule, we called Kate. Whenever I'd be plowing with her, she'd set the pace, deciding when to take a break even in the middle of a row of corn. She'd simply stop. So I'd sit down and take a break also. She wouldn't go again even with clods of dirt thrown at her haunches. When she'd decide to go back to work, she'd start plowing without a plowman. I'd jump up and start plowing also.

We had a young horse, Prince, who had barely been broken. But he was a beautiful middle-sized sorrel. He was wonderful to work with, quite cooperative. He had one problem that he and I had to accommodate. When he was much younger he had been caught in a tangle of barbed wire, which had been left in the pasture where he grazed. The wire had scratched and cut him up so badly that whenever a metal wire or chain would touch his legs, he'd panic.

I'd be real careful with the trace chains, which had to be fastened to the hames and collar in order for him to pull a plow. Prince was also a good riding horse.

Prince and I were a good team, particularly in breaking ground. The turning plow would have to plow counter-clockwise, because the plow would turn the soil to the right. The horse and plowman would start at the outer edge, and each round would get smaller and smaller.

Actually not rounds, but squares. At the end of one side, it's "Whoa, Haw". Prince would then stop, turn left and proceed to the end of that side. We would follow that routine until we met ourselves in the middle of the field when we had finished.

I once overheard Daddy tell Mamma, "Reid can plow a straight furrow." There was pride in his voice, but he couldn't afford to tell me that he was pleased that I could plow so well. There's something about fathers and sons. My physical therapist gives me more compliments than my dad ever did.

One of the fields I plowed has raised two crops of pine trees since then.

We had a horse for awhile, who was a stump-sucker. That was a bigger problem for him than the eggs had been a problem for a suck-egg dog. The stump-sucker would chew on the wooden edges of his feeding trough, and in doing so would get wood fibers in his throat and become wheezy. He couldn't work very well then. A simple solution was to cover the edge of his trough with tin to prevent any more chewing.

We had a wonderful old horse, named Dan. He wasn't very strong to begin with, so we didn't have him do the hard pulling. He became rather ill, having a hard time even standing up. Daddy knew that Ol' Dan wouldn't live very long. We were going to be gone for the weekend, so I tried to feed Ol' Dan. But he didn't eat much or drink much water.

As soon as we got back at the end of the second day, Ott and I went running to check on Ol' Dan. He seemed unable to move. I sat in his stall in such a way that I could hold his head in my lap. He rolled his large eyes toward me then took a breath, closed his eyes and stopped breathing.

Ol' Dan had died.

Ott and I cried a little. We had lost a friend. We felt even worse, when we realized what was going to happen with the body.

We had seen dead people in coffins, but we knew they wouldn't be getting a coffin for our horse. What they did was to fasten a log chain around Dan's chest and hook the chain to the doodlebug tractor. Then the carcass was pulled down into the woods to a gully that needed to be filled. After depositing him there they threw dirt on him. I checked on him occasionally after that, and had to throw on more dirt as the foxes and raccoons had been digging to get to him, and he could no longer kick back.

I've already introduced the reader to the living doodlebug. I should explain what a doodlebug tractor is. The name of course is taken from the living ant lion larva. The tractor was just an old '33 Chevy chassis with a truck rear end, including the axle and wheels of a truck. It was replacing the horse for pulling wagons, logs and drag pans for scooping dirt. Of course it had to have two men working it, as it had no hydraulic equipment. So one person had to drive and another to man the device like a dragpan. As I had not yet learned to drive, I was the point person on the scoop. What a terrible job. I would get all the exhaust from the tractor, and if it hit a snag like a root or a rock, the back end would upend. I had to be extra cautious and dodge the end of the dragpan or it would catch me right under the chin.

Several times when I was driving too casually and showing off at how easily I could shift gears, I missed second and threw it up into reverse instead. The tractor would lurch backward. It's a wonder that I didn't tear out the clutch or strip some gears.

Of course the transition from horse power to doodlebug power wasn't always as smooth as one would like.

Though I'm not of a nerdy technological mind,
I didn't think technology could be so unkind.
    It's the rage
    This digital age
Leaving this old farm boy way, way behind.

My friend, Jesse Wilkins, wasn't really slow.
For his first driving lesson, he was all aglow.
    When the car left the road,
    As his dad told,
Jesse was yelling , "Whoa, Nellie, Whoa."

Methodist Stones

Someone, knowing of my interest in stone work, told me of a competition in England of laying a dry wall (meaning no mortar) of stone. The contestants were given a pile of rocks, which they were to use building a free-standing wall ... not a retaining wall.

In order to build a substantial wall, an occasional "Methodist" stone was necessary.

"What is a Methodist stone?"

"It's two-faced. It must span the width of the wall in order to hold each side. Otherwise the wall wouldn't stand. One of the sides would cave in without the anchor stones, tying the two sides together."

This intrigued me, so I told my Aunt Myrtle Esther Hoots (a good Methodist) about the contest and the importance of Methodist stones.

She was incensed. "We Methodists are not two-faced."

"Aunt Myrtle, just think that even if it's true that we Methodists are two-faced, at least we hold things together ... two different sides."

She did pause in silent thought. It was just prior to a national election.

She brightened, as she gave her verdict: "Maybe we ought to send more Methodists to Congress. Someone needs to reach to the other side."

Not a bad idea. Let's do it.

Health Issues

We had health problems from time to time. It was amazing that we didn't have more health issues, as we stayed so close to each other, particularly in winter, when we huddled close to the heat source, whether it was the kitchen cook stove or the fireplace.

Another questionable factor was our water situation. Whenever Daddy or I would bring water from the spring, we'd put the bucket of water on a small table in the kitchen. A dipper was kept in the bucket for dipping out water for cooking or for drinking. After one of us would drink water out of the dipper, we'd put the dipper back in the bucket for the next thirsty soul. Perhaps instead of sharing disease with sharing the dipper, we developed and shared immunity.

All three of us kids had had the measles before we moved to Baux Mountain However I caught the mumps when I was in the fourth grade.

That was the first time I had missed a day of school. I cried when the school bus picked up my siblings. Ott thought how silly of me to cry over missing school. He would welcome an opportunity to miss a couple weeks of school.

As a matter of fact, he tried his darndest to get

the mumps from me. We had to share a bed. Daddy always came to our bed in the morning to pick up Ott and take him into the kitchen where it was warm near the kitchen-stove fire.

When both Dad and Ott thought that Ott had caught the mumps, Daddy would pick him up and ask, "How's my little man feeling this morning?"

Of course, Ott would then say, "I don' feel so good." He'd then moan a couple of times for good measure. He never got the mumps, much to his dismay. One night for some reason, Ott and I changed where we slept in the bed. The next morning when Daddy came to get Ott he mistakenly picked up me. When he got to the light and saw his mistake, he put me down in a hurry, almost dropping his "little man".

A year later, Ott got seriously sick. When Daddy took him to the hospital, he had to be carried on a pillow, because it was so extremely painful to be touched on any part of his body.

That night I went to stay at Uncle John's. We didn't get to bed until nearly midnight. When I said my nighttime prayer, I prayed fervently, Please, Dear God, make my little brother well again. Don't let him die."

Daddy stayed with Ott that night in the hospital. He had taken a ham sandwich with him for a snack. After Ott went to sleep, Daddy decided to have his snack. But when he took a bite, something was wrong. It felt like something in his mouth was biting him. He had turned the light off, in order for Ott to sleep. When he turned on the light he saw that the sandwich was invaded by ants. They were having their snack of the sandwich and the inside of Daddy's mouth.

Daddy rinsed out his mouth about the same time Ott woke up in terrible pain. He said that all the pain had gone to one foot. Daddy, wanting to help if he could, said, "Son, do you think it would help if I rubbed your foot?"

"I think so."

Daddy massaged his foot and gradually the pain began to subside The time was about midnight, when I was praying for my little brother. The next day they came home. Ott was sitting up in the car.

He had rheumatic fever, which would occasionally inflict a lot of pain again. On one such episode he was hallucinating and thought a train was about to run over him.

We all thought he was dying. We were standing around his bed when he said to Daddy, "Will somebody take care of my chickens when I'm gone?"

Daddy looked at me and barked, "Go and water his chickens. Don't you love your brother anymore?" I was devastated, not only over Ott's situation, but I felt that Daddy was being cruel to me for no purpose.

I did water his chickens, not only with good spring water but also with my tears. Ott survived, but always had a rheumatic heart after that.

When I was 11 and Ott was nine, we both had our tonsils removed. The folks were especially concerned about Ott, because of his heart. They were afraid that he may not survive.

We shared the same hospital room. After the surgeries, Ott was awake and doing fine, when they wheeled me in. Mamma was standing by his bed. He said, "Has Reid gone crazy?" I apparently was trying to climb the wall and singing Amazing Grace.

We both survived.

Susie was healthy during this period. She later started RN training at Presbyterian Hospital in Charlotte. I think one of the reasons she chose to become a nurse was because she was so impressed with a nurse, Miss Lewis, who was our nurse when we were in the hospital.

However, Susie came home and said she

wasn't going back. Apparently she was not doing well. On a Sunday afternoon Daddy drove up to the Crowders' and called Dr. Fritz in Walkertown, 15 miles away. He came, interviewed Susie and asked Daddy to step out into the yard. Our house was terribly small; not a place for a private talk.

He explained to Daddy what was wrong and suggested what needed to be done. It turns out there were two Susies and one Susie was getting demerits meant for the other one. Her issue was cleared up. She earned an RN and became a registered nurse. We had a younger cousin, Eddie Burcham, who thought RN meant Runny Nose.

By the way, we didn't have insurance in those days. For the Sunday afternoon house call, Dr. Fritz charged $5.

In the spring of 1942, Mamma got real fat and had to go to the hospital. She recovered and came home with a baby girl, Mary Evelyn.

Ott cried. He said that he was so worried about Mamma. Susie and I teased him. "You weren't worried about Mamma. You're not going to be the baby in the family any longer." The aunts and uncles continued calling him Baby Ott.

Other than the mumps, my health issues had been minimum, until in the summer of 1941.

It was annual revival meeting time at the church. During one of the evening services, my stomach started hurting terribly. I was sitting by Daddy in the pew, and told him that I had a horrible stomach ache. He thought it was from something I ate for supper and would ease with some medicine when we got home.
He changed his mind when I stretched out on the pew from such pain. He knew I would never ordinarily do such a thing unless I had an unusual problem. There was no sleep that night. The next morning Daddy took me to see Dr. Voss, who had operated on Daddy for a burst appendix, several years earlier.

Dr. Voss went into action immediately and told us to meet him at the hospital. Miss Lewis checked us in. The pain was still there, but somewhat mitigated by the diversions all around me.

Pretty soon I was on a gurney ... I didn't know what it was except a table with wheels. In the operating room, they put something over my mouth and told me to breathe. I was already breathing, but I obliged by taking a big gulp of air.

Immediately I was at the top of the operating room with all those bright lights and shiny metal utensils.

In about five minutes (at least it seemed like

five maybe six minutes) I was in a bed with everything white around me; sheets, nurse, my nightgown, a big white bandage across my stomach.

It was unusually hot even in dog days of July. The old Winston Salem City Hospital didn't have air conditioning in those days. Mamma was standing by the bed, looking very sad, and Susie stood next to her.

The whole experience was so fantastic, that I asked Mamma, "Have I died and gone to heaven?"

Even more seriously she said, "Do you think it's going to be this hot in Heaven?'

Uh Oh! I've gone to the wrong place. I was trapped. I knew that when the altar call had been made each night, I should have answered the invitation and avoided eternal damnation. Now it was too late.

Mamma hadn't meant to alarm me or even to make a joke. She had wanted to assure me that I wasn't dead. She had no clue what incessant mental wrestling I'd been in all week.

Then I made an intelligent mental discovery. Mamma certainly wouldn't be in the kingdom of the devil.

I didn't say any more about dying.

Susie wanted to be comforting in some way, so with a sourpuss expression she chatted, "Reid, do you have any cards?" How did she think cards could be there that quickly. "She looked so deliberately serious, that I started laughing. That hurt.

She went immediately into self-defense mode. "Mamma I didn't mean to make him laugh. I'm so sorry, Reid, to make you laugh. "
It became evident that Mamma had warned her about making me laugh.

As her demeanor became even more anxious, I really did "split a gut".

I recovered and so did Sister Susie.

All in all, we were a pretty healthy family

—X—

The Spring

The spring water has already been introduced with the moving day rambling and wading in the spring water. Actually, at that time we were just about 80 yards below the spring.

When the first settlers came to these hills, they had two considerations for plans for building their houses. The first issue would be a road, as it was the way in and out.

The next consideration was the spring, which provided the fluid lifeline to the household and the activities of its inhabitants. Usually, it was a bit of a compromise between the road and the spring, but some houses were built a long distance from the road, near a good water supply. The children in those houses would have to walk a long way to the road to catch the school bus.

Our house was close to the road and about 50 yards from the spring ... downhill. I often wondered why the Good Lord hadn't put the spring uphill. Then we could carry the water downhill and only empty buckets uphill.

Keeping the water supply in the house was one of my chores. If I carried one bucket, it would slosh water all over my legs, as I would need to lean away from the weight of the water in order to balance myself and my burden. Ergo, I would carry two buckets, which not only provided a balance, but also provided extra water with the extra bucket.

Anyone, who has not carried water (uphill) from a spring, is unaware of how much water is used and for how many purposes. We always needed drinking water, so a bucket of water would be placed on a table in the kitchen. It would have a dipper in it, so that anyone, needing a drink of water, would dip the dipper into the water then drink directly from the dipper, before putting it back in the water for the next thirsty soul. Folks, nowadays, would cringe at such a bad hygiene practice.

Of course, Mamma had to have plenty of water for cooking. I would put a couple of gallons into the reservoir, which was a container in the woodstove, on the other end from the firebox.

Just a few words about the stove. I had to keep enough wood in the wood box for cooking. If it was insufficient, I got no lunch ... nor did anyone else. The stove was wonderful for cooking. If the cook wanted a super hot fire, s/he would place the pan or pot right over the firebox. The stove lids could be lifted out and a pot could be placed in the opening, right over the flame. For less heat, the cooking container would be placed farther from the firebox. Placed about three feet over the stove was a warming oven, quite convenient for biscuits or other food, needing only warming. The oven was right next to the firebox and was wonderful after the cook knew its quirks and potential.

Back to the spring. Water was needed also for washing clothes in the winter. Also baths were needed weekly, and a galvanized tub was put on the stove. When the water was hot enough, two people would hold rings on each side of the tub and put it on the floor near the firebox end of the stove. It would be put there so that the bather would be at the warmest part of the kitchen.

The weekly bathing ritual would take place Saturday night after supper and the dish-washing. The kitchen would then become the bathroom ... literally. The baths would begin first with the youngest and ending with Mamma and then Daddy. All bathers would use the same water, because of the toil bringing all that water, not only for the baths, but also for the other uses already mentioned.

In the summer time the bath water was warmed differently. The tub was placed outside on Saturday morning, then after filling it with water it was left outside for the sun to warm the water. A kind of cloth fence was erected around the tub to provide a bit of privacy for the bather.

Our spring was about halfway between our house and the Taylors. In fact, our deed said that the property line went through the middle of the spring. Whenever anyone wanted a cool drink of water, the thirsty one would go to the spring, where the water came directly from the cool clay earth.

One day Daddy was plowing not far from the spring. I believe I was in the apple tree. He yelled, "Reid, go get me a drink of water from the spring." The way he told it was, "I had kept plowing and after a while, Reid came sauntering across the field, whistling. I yelled, 'Reid, where's my water?' He stopped whistlin' and said, 'I forgot the bucket.'" That was when they started calling me the "absent-minded professor".

Our city cousins couldn't abide the idea of drinking water that had just trickled out of dirt and stayed in a basin carved out of stone. They knew also that the basin was never cleaned, except when a lot of leaves had dropped into the spring in the fall and had to be dipped out. They preferred that warm city spigot water, which had chemicals and I don't know what-n-all.

When I was in the hospital for an appendectomy, Daddy was so concerned, he would have done anything for me. He said,

"Son, what can I get for you?" I knew he would get me anything, even ice cream, which was usually a wonderful treat. It didn't take long for me to claim my offered gift. "Daddy, would you bring some Baux Mountain spring water? I can't stand this stuff."

Even though the spring held a substance that I had to carry up a hill, that same water was greatly appreciated when compared to other options.

Daddy fixed a wooden hinged box, which didn't have a bottom. It was placed in the water just below the spring. That was where jugs of milk were put, to keep it cool as long as possible. We didn't have a refrigerator, as we were living beyond the power lines.

————————————————— X —————————————————

An Extra Methodist Story

My mother was a very modest, but avid Methodist, as was her beloved father, Frank Winfrey Brinkley. He died of Rocky Mountain Spotted Fever, when Mamma, the oldest of eight children, was 18 years old. Grandpa sang most of the night before he passed away. The songs seemed to be favorites in his local Methodist church.

Some years later, we had friends ... I'll call them the Smiths ... who were also Methodist. Many years later, after I had left North Carolina, Mamma wrote me that she met Mrs. Smith in town. Apparently, Mrs. Smith wanted to tell Mamma all about her church (not Methodist).

As I read further, I could tell that my dear, quiet mother was getting angrier and angrier. The way Mrs. Smith continued to share her new-found religion, she seemed to be looking for a new convert. She confessed that she had never known Jesus, really, and, "didn't feel saved in the grace of God, before I accepted Christ in the revival meeting in the Holy Ghost Church of God ... certainly not sanctified as long as I was a Methodist."

That was too much for Mamma. When Mrs. Smith dropped the key word, "Methodist",

Mamma responded for the first time. "All that may be true, but at least we Methodists are humble."

Mamma was proud of her modest Methodist heritage, and no one deserved the title more than she ... my proudly humble Methodist mother.

www.ingramcontent.com/pod-product-compliance
Lightning Source LLC
Chambersburg PA
CBHW071503140726
47997CB00005B/1837

Beyond the Power Lines

E. Reid Gilbert

A3D Impressions

Tucson / Minneapolis

POEMS

E. Reid Gilbert

Beyond the Power Lines of the Heart

A3D Impressions

Tucson / Minneapolis

Published by

A3D Impressions
P.O. Box 14181, Tucson, AZ 85732
www.a3dimpressions.com
a3dimpressions@gmail.com

Publisher's Cataloging-in-Publication data

Names: Gilbert, E. Reid, author.
Title: Beyond the power lines / E. Reid Gilbert.
Description: Tucson, AZ; Minneapolis, MN: A3D Impressions, 2022.
Identifiers: LCCN: 2022912383 | ISBN: 979-8-9864049-0-5
Subjects: LCSH American poetry--21st century. | Grief--Poetry. | Essays.
| BISAC POETRY / General POETRY / American / General | POETRY
/ Subjects & Themes / Death, Grief, Loss | POETRY / Subjects &
Themes / Places
Classification: LCC PS3607 .I42243 B49 2022 | DDC 811.6

Special thanks to Judith Holt
for assistance in editing.

Contents

--- ✀ ---

HEART STRINGS

These poems are plucked with heart strings
   Strumming blues and joy as the heart sings
     With challenges and sensors.
     Questions with no answers;
Experiences, which the fullness of life brings.

Now a nonagenarian with roots in those days
Rainy days as well as those filled with sun rays.
     Rambling the woods and the creeks,
     Part-time jobs lasting for weeks.
Daily chores, but still enough time left to play.

1.
PEOPLE

An old fellow

An old fellow in New York celebrated his new U.S. citizenship today.

> When have you celebrated your citizenship?

A young couple in Tucson will take their wedding vows tomorrow.

> Have you lately shared your wedding vows?

A mother in WV welcomed a new baby last week.

> Have you recently sung goodnight songs to your little ones?

A family in NC two weeks ago welcomed a brother released from prison.

> Have you lately told your siblings that you love them?

A grieving Wisconsin family celebrated the life of their departed matriarch.

> Have you called Grandad recently?

It's never too late and certainly not too early.

To Stand ... Erect

Looking not for sympathy, empathy nor pity,
I'll tell you a tale in Tucson City.
I don't mean to complain nor even to whine
On a November day I fractured my spine.

A cataclysmic catastrophe in my universe,
For this scene I was unable to rehearse.
Hospitals, rehabs, nurses and doctors
Orderlies, counselors and pill concoctors.
In the painful months of my slow recovery,
I made a strange, but productive discovery.

As comfortable as my wheelchair was for me,
To sit there in comfort was not meant to be.
To be seated and there for an hour remain,
To try to stand then causes a great deal of pain.
To avoid the pain requires physical activity,
Resulting in welcome unexpected productivity.

In a similar manner, a matter left unspoken,
Is that our American spine has also been broken.
We can sit here and moan about the pandemic
To leave it at that is simply academic.

We must stand up to the plagues beset upon us;
The political fracture and the coronavirus.
The president tried then with his usual
    pretension
To give the election an illegal extension.

Boasting and posturing seemed to be endemic,
Atop all that was the covid-19 pandemic.
We're divided with unfair racial disparity,
Instead of integrity with inclusive clarity.
This is just too much this double health hit
Both warn us not to linger too long and sit.
They're so new we don't know how to behave
We're tempted to crawl back into our personal
    cave.

We can't gather now in compatible crowds
Even with causes magnificently endowed.
Virtual reality must now be sufficient
While being neither clueless nor omniscient.

In this virtual reality, it's enticing to be simply
    bored.
We must remain engaged until health is
    restored.

We may be on an unpaved road to recovery
When to stand upright is a healthy discovery.

Not just to stand, but to stand up erect,
Stand up for lasting, healing effect.
For both personal and social regained health,
Which is finally our only actual wealth.

Sitting too long may come with great cost.
The ability to stand may forever be lost.

Now after incisive scalpel and connecting suture
We awaken to a promising yet undetermined
    future.

A Letter

Dear Sister Maya,

I started this letter to you this evenin'
Even though now you be gone from us
An' I dare say that anyone what reads your letter
    to us and the caged bird
won't be able to hold back a tear

For another reason for a tear
Me, a white southern boy, for sharing in the
    shame of southern white men
whether in the klan or just standin' idly by
The southern Black mamma for feelin' the pain
    of hidin' her biddies
from the chicken hawks, circlin' lazy overhead
The Black men for not bein' able or not choosin'
    to stay

An' those folks north of the mason's an' dixon's
    line
for finally, maybe, understand that you've
    regarded us below the line as, at best, simply
    slow
and at worst vicious creatures
worthy only to provide some good weather for
    visitin'
or cheap products from our grimy mills
provided by cheap labor of gnarled hands

Get Out of the Way

the artist arrives
just in time
to disappear
as the image advances
in color and form
while music dances
on its own staff of aural waves

somehow the words
emerge out of the haze
of inconclusions
which the writer
simply manipulates
in his ability
to place on the blank page

the canvas calls for
the attention of the oil
daubed by
the nimble fingers of
a child
who knows
instinctively
how
to imprint

the art and
the event
conjoin and
conspire
to transport
the recipient
into the
moment
of
divine light
beyond the vanishing point

so get out of the way

A Lifetime

It seems a lifetime.
And so it has been.
What has happened to it?
Where has it gone?
What did it amount to?
What did it accomplish?

Let's ask questions of the questions.
What did it need to accomplish?
Was it expected to amount to anything?
Where was it supposed to go?
Go where?
That was the earlier question.
Was something assumed to happen?

Hamlet had the appropriate question;
To be or not to be?
Isn't it sufficient merely to be
Or not?

------------------------------✄------------------------------

A New Encounter

What does that person want from me?

What does he expect from me?

What does he need from me?

What do I want from him?

What do I need from him?

The answer in both directions:
     VALIDATION

-------------------------------- ✄ --------------------------------

Life Begins at Eighty
or
Life Begins to End at Eighty

Toward the end
        dimensions dance
        time fluctuates
                the spirit flutters
                        no pity for tomorrow

Compassion
        for one's self
                and those others
                        along the path
                        way

One doesn't need to
        see the depot
                to know the train is
                        pulling into the station

The scenery creeps by
        the tunnel darkens
                the brakes squeal painfully
                        lurching to a stop

Welcoming hosts
        waiting on the platform
                are still
                        another story

Living On

'Tis often said that our immortality,
If such there is,
Dwells in the continued
Lives and values of our children.

To say "children" is also to include
Those students and co-laborers
For whom we have had some
Earthly responsibility.

What continues to prevail
Is not the blood, bones and sinews
Of this human vessel,
But the divine spirit in each of us.

If immortality is actual,
It is this spark which, hopefully,
Is kindled anew
In each new generation.

Even though the pitcher be broken
And the shards scattered or buried,
The essence of pitcher with its function
Lives on in new form,

Shaped by the skilled hands
Of another potter
With newly acquired clay
Rekindled in a renewed flame.

When Meeting Becomes

When meeting becomes
    A pattern
When pattern becomes
    A habit
When habit becomes
    A ritual
When ritual becomes religion
    Dogma is born
Dogma begets priests
Priests become authorities
    who hold the keys
The keys dangle
    before the mere humans
Who wallow in
    Self-deprecation
Leading to an
    Early grave
        Self-delivered
           or not

The Colored Families

The colored families live quite amicably
Side by side on NO EXIT street.
The White family and the Black family
Live in the neighborhood of Bright Leaf Drive.
Louise Black is the best friend of Irene White.
And of course, vice versa.
The confusion occurs when you learn
That the Blacks are white and the Whites are
    black.
To be specific, Louise Black is white and Irene
    White is black.

The Grays live the next street over.
I believe the Greens moved away last fall.
The Browns have moved in where the Greens
    used to live.
The Blues stop by every once in a while.
The Peacocks strut by on Sunday mornings.
We seem to see the Roses every summer.
It's rumored that the Greens will be returning
    soon.

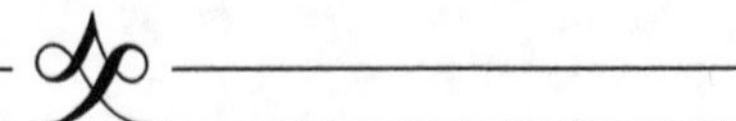

2.
TIME
and PLACE

Time and Space

The past presses ever on my present
While the future constantly interferes
With no time to be present
As each moment moves on
Before the now can be known.

What's out there is still unknown
Until the inner space is researched
Requiring some outer exploration
To understand even minutely
The innerscape of here.

These interstices of time and space
Create the dimensions
Of life as I experience it
Innate in boy and man
Breathing the ether of reality.

Mountains Gesture

Mountains are not simply sleeping giants,
    Even foothills like Baux Mountain
        Aren't napping.

Mt. Etna spews ash and lava into the heavens
    Lighting up the night skies
        For Mediterranean sailors.

Pilot Mountain thrusts herself from the floor
    of the Piedmont
        Standing as a sentinel for many tribes
            Over countless ages.

Mt. Rushmore celebrates our national leaders
    Enticing curious travelers
        From all edges of the country.

Mt. Everest challenges the hardy souls
    Daring them to embrace
        Her peak experiences.

The Sauratown Mountains beckon hikers
    To scale over the shoulders
        Of Hanging Rock Park.

Baux Mountain reminds this old schoolboy
    Where life was centered
        From which to view the whole
        world.

---❦---

The Eleventh Hour 5/11/21 11:11 pm

The day light is nearly finished,
Darkest night is drawing nigh.
The nighthawk doth hover,
As the last hours go flying by.

The midnight hour will soon be here
Past the day's omissions and commissions;
Some things to bemoan and others to cheer.
Pay close attention to each of the transitions.
11:30
The eleventh hour has great significance;
    Looking ahead and what has gone before.
For some it may be the last/lost chance
To dance through the swinging door.

———————————— ❧ ————————————

Midnight

for some and various reasons
I lay awake and couldn't
sleep
at midnight
the world is embroiled in
a cosmic destructive
problem
at midnight
many places of business
and institutions
are closing
at midnight
I'm not speaking here of
the horrible pandemic
of coronavirus
at midnight
it's the greed and fear
of selfish interests
of people
at midnight
it seems we are caught
in the miasma of
the quicksand
of midnight
the clock is slowly
but insistently
clicking
PAST MIDNIGHT

The Final Touch

I could share with you the initial opening
Or the evolving circumstances that led to decay.
The personalities emerging from the text
May engage your attention for a while.

The roads taken or not taken may elicit
Certain images in your mind.
The descriptive bends on the road
Or in the river I could describe in some detail.

But the final touch is sacrosanct
And it's not possible for me to reveal
Oh I could tell you how it ends
But one must earn the final release.

It Is No Surprise

It is no surprise nor should it be
That woes beset us along the way.
It is no surprise nor should it be
That joys are given to us each day.

Of how we encounter each of these gifts.
Is not just a matter of circumstance
Gifts they are, whether earned or not
Much more than matters of happenstance.

With each new moment comes a challenge
Of how we respond to these lessons of life.
And lessons whether recognized as such
Certainly the joys as well as the strife.

So we muddle on as best we can,
Swept along in the flooded streams
Trying to find substance partially lived
Other than our fantasies or daydreams.

There comes a time soon or late
when everything turns upside down
and we struggle to make everything fit
into a dogmatic form
which seemed to have served us well
up until now
so we bobble along
like baubles in a bubble bath.
but we wonder anew
if the water we're in
is given to sustain us
or end our misery
we push/pull squeeze/expand
we find that the best we can do
is keep our head above water
then if opportunity presents itself
we may swim toward shore
That depends of course
if we've learned
how to swim.

Within and Beyond

Beyond Baux Mountain
    There is Pilot Knob.
But within Baux Mountain
    Who knows?
        The rocks we dug for our new house
        more then sixty years ago!
        But is there nothing more than the
        striated stone yielding to the mason's
        chisel?

When we return to the moment
    The flatness disappears
        Or does it'?

What is it that we see
    That we hear
    That we feel
    That we smell
    That we touch?
        And what is it that touches us?

The fish are immersed in the depth of the ocean,
    While we may be lost in the depths of grief.
But if the ocean deep sustain the fish
        Why do the sorrowing challenges
        dislodge our belief?

The secret presence of that which lies under the ground
The unknown character of that which waits beyond the horizon
The mysteries unfolding in the invisible atmosphere, itself
     Genius loci
     The particular power of place.

To Write

To write of one's life

Is to live it again?

To remember the cast?

And re-member oneself

To a time gone by?

A long time back

Or only yesterday.

Can the recalled kiss

Be as fresh today,

As when I was fresh

With the nubile you

That honeysuckled night?

The agony now to write

Is the long look back

The Days Ahead

The days ahead
May be filled with dread,
But hope instead
Could be the thread
Which leads to patience and understanding
And reluctance to sound an alarm
We strengthen our focus
In hopes to avoid any harm.

Which Way

Which way to look
        Now in my decaying dotage
Approaching the end
        Of my eighth decade?

Often looking back
        I don't always recall
Not always wanting
        To remember it all.

Can I look ahead to
        Tomorrow but then
Realize I shouldn't try
        To project any further?

Would it have helped
        If the gifter would have giv' me
A way to know how long
        I was to endure?

I could look to the side
        To see fellow creatures;
Look down to earth and come to know
        That will soon be my bed.

Looking up would be nothing new
        For I've always gazed
At the clouds
        And the stars.

Those daydreams gazing
        Out the school room windows
Dare I now hope for
        Clouds of heavenly journeys?

Today is Yesterday's Future

Today is yesterday's future.
Today will be tomorrow's past.
Today is today's present.

What have you done with yesterday's
    future?
When will you finish tomorrow's past?
What are you doing with today's present?

Is today a clone of yesterday?
Will tomorrow be a clone of today?
Will it be a choice?

There is no time like the present
There is no time but the present

Compounding your time line
Of past, present and future
What is required of today?
That you be present.
Your presence
Is needed
Totally!
Present.

The Year
Has Come and Gone

The year has come and gone
And where are we?
You're there & I'm here
Wherever here or there might be.

The space between us is simply air
Whether 6 inches or a million miles
All is transcended in the misty fog
By a loving glance or a gentle smile.

It's ironic when measuring time or space
Space separating clime from clime
But as we step happily into the new year,
We step together at the very same time.

The Years

When years creep up
        age pounces suddenly
onto one's consciousness
        and the cards begin to fall.

It's lonely enough
        when others forget who you are.
it's utterly devastating
        when you are in search of you.

The search didn't open up
        just this morning
when I began to reflect
        on my eighty some years.

Time after time it happened
        every time I fell in love
but even more so when
        love didn't seem enough.

Beware of what I wished for
        the lies we tell ourselves ... and one
            another
the fictions we make of other people
        caught between grace and ghastly.

Lasting Impressions
of barbourville ky from the '50s

The Folks

Overheard in the super market,
"I can't do a thing with these avercados.
I've cooked them ever which way
and they never taste right."

One wonderful kindly neighbor
was too often taken to drink.
A few days after a late night binge
with "the boys" he lost his hat.
He received the hat at the post office,
nicely wrapped with a beautifully
handwritten note,
"Thanks, George, for a lovely evening."
The boys made sure they were close by
    when he received his lost hat after his
    lost evening.

The Students

My students were from various parts of
the country, but the most memorable
were from the mountains.
One high school girl from Rose Hill,
Virginia came to the college on senior
visitation day and stepped out on our
tiny stage and said, "I'm going to be an
actress."
and she was and did,
one of the best acting students I had there
or in many institutions after that.

Another student from Harlan, Kentucky
wrote and published an unauthorized
underground paper, satirizing some of
the college activities and students and
faculty.
When he got to class late I congratulated
him as I felt that his underground
epistle was one of the most interesting
things I had experienced there.
He later informed me that he had just
come from the president's office where
he was reprimanded and threatened
with expulsion if he continued his
excursion into unapproved journalism.
He also said that he had almost quit
college that day of his own accord.

However he continued his journalism
    career beyond college,winning many
    awards at the Dayton, Ohio Daily News.
When years later I was in touch with that
    president, I asked him if he was in
    touch with any of the former students.
"Oh, yes! I keep in regular touch with the
    boy from Harlan.
He's had quite an illustrious career in
    journalism. Did you know?"
"Oh yes! And it began at Union College.
    Did you know?"

The Language

When my wife, who was not from the
     mountains, returned to the house after
     a short trip to the store she was
     fuming.
"I can't understand these people."
"Why? What did they say?"
"This fellow says, 'Whu fer ye?' He kept
     repeating it and I said, 'I don't know
     what you're saying, but I came to buy a
     broom.'"
"What he was saying was 'What for you?'"
In an Oral Interpretation of Literature class
     a naîve Kentucky boy read badly a
     poem written by an African American
     writer.
In my response I suggested that "We have
     to be careful when we read the dialect
     of another culture, so that we aren't
     parodying it."
In his best Kentucky mountain accent he
     said, "Mr. Gilbert, isn't it strange now
     that there are so many dialects out
     there, and we don't have any?"
It was all I could do to keep a New Jersey
     boy from pummeling my Kentucky
     student.

3.
IDEAS

The Idea and the Word

The beauty of an idea
The magic of a word.
Which do you suppose
Precedes the other
And which carries more weight
In the scheme of things?

Some words of course are uttered
Without intention or thought.
And then again there's the idea
That may never be expressed.

But when the two power on
In a shared conjugal moment
The world may celebrate
Or cringe back into a cave.

What looms ahead now
For us and the world?

Does anyone have an idea?
And what's the word?

Really, what is the word
And the idea behind it?

The Soul Searches Beyond

Beyond everyday survival needs
The soul ever searches
Past the hedonistic senses of this earthly life
Undergirding the pleasure of love and feast
Well above the pain of fear and loss
The consciousness strives to grow.

A storm is sensed out there somewhere
Signaled by streaks of lightning
Piercing the line of the horizon
One always wonders if the storm
Will bring sustaining water for thirsty throats
And grateful crops
Or floods instead
Deluging our valleys
Sweeping away the amassed past
Even the detritus of abandoned hopes.

Desperately
The old man hangs on
To memories
He can sometimes recount.

---✄---

Silence of the Words

From whence cometh these words
    These silent words

Which I read on the papyrus
    or write on the page
Distracting me from
    other chores ...

The writer hasn't told me
    the origin of the word ... His word
    or even its intention ... Its mission

Perhaps even more puzzling
    is the genesis of the words
        my words
    Born perhaps
        in my inner psyche
            to reflect a hidden past pain
        or rather
        to express an unexpressed
    yearning need

And yet
    still yet
        there they are
            which I see ... these silent words

They must not remain thus
        SILENT
They yearn to be voiced
        reverberating this time
        on the tympanum
        to join the visual word
                having already arrived

There ... In the midst
                of my consciousness
        the visual word ... embraces
        the audible word

And then they dance
        oh they dance ... to the music of the
        celestial choir

When the word thus
        soothes me to rest or ... challenges me to
        action

Perhaps to lead me
        with new words ... voiced
        in expanded
                renewed worlds
        and further
                lively moments ...

Of this life time

Of War

The joke or joy of war belies
The horror or honor of battles.
The destruction/dishonor violates
The valor/value of the fight.
The personal distress hides from
The national distinction of combat.
The skirmish exhilaration hastens to
The resounding explosion of limbs,
The recruit anticipation of hope is shadowed by
The shattered veteran anxiety of war.

Next time families of politicians
Must man the guns,
While families of CEOs
Must nab the snipers.
Then all will share equally
The bounty of the final moment.
The cornucopia of war profits with
The overloads for the morticians
As well as the warlords.

In Reaching Out

In reaching out
        Must we close inward
As we use abstruse language
        Or corporate buzzwords
Only to identify with our playground group
        As well as to let others know we're special?
They're not currently welcome
        Until they learn our language
Or follow a specific academic track
        Perhaps to sleep with one of the innies.

We all wait to know what it really means
        In narrative terms
When we attend the performance
        Or observe the art
Just try to listen to the trekkers
        And try to decipher their jargon
Or eavesdrop on the bikers
        Without getting squelched
For even the Cajuns have their own
        Particular mixed language.

Is it that only the insiders qualify
        Because they're the ones in the know
While the aliens must shiver aside
        Standing out in the ice-crusted snow?

———————————— ✎ ————————————

Death Lurks

Death sits
Like a gargoyle
On the parapet
Of a gothic cathedral
Seemingly waiting

He doesn't wait

He lurks

For his opportunity
To have the last word
Of this life
Of mine.

He does have the last word
Of this go round
But I believe,
Which he doesn't understand.

So I wait
We wait
We all wait

In our living/dying
Existence,

While he lurks
Greeting us
Constantly
With a Cheshire cat
Grin.

Getting It Right

just get it right
the expectations
of everyone

but especially my own
can I own the expectations
or have I won a reprieve from my own
to do this or maybe that
perhaps a middle road
would be best

under the happenstances
but do happenstances
alter the values
or consequences
of expectations

is there any hope

....

really

A Murmuring Light Ahead?

Having carelessly toted my load
   I grope down this unfamiliar road,
      Darkness ominously thickens.

Seeing only a few feet ahead,
    Further from my cherished dream.
      I'm now lost; will I ever get home?

The question is now all I've got
    On a snowy evening or not
      What road do I take?

Whenever the question calls
    Through the blizzard squalls,
      Will you listen to the lesson?

There is now little choice
    As I hear a muted voice.
      Uneasily I continue forward.

Is that a flickering light beckoning me?
    To the scene I've known before,
      Through an ever-changing door?

SO I LISTEN
    To the inner vibrating river
Beside the centered creative flame
    And there my truth abides,
Somewhere in the ever-embracing light of life.

I'll Wait

I've been waiting
For quite a while
But for what
And for whom?

I waited for Godot
     And for the cows to come home
Neither materialized
     Or at least I didn't recognize them at the
     time.

But my time for waiting is running out
I've reached my four score years and seven.

You don't use time to wait

You wait with spirit
The heart waits.

Are you still waiting?

Glimpses

We catch glimpses
Not necessarily in poetic form or narrative prose
But thoughts and images which seem
to impel one forward at times
while looking back
or within

so bring your self
actually everything you have

no schedules, plans, political concerns other than
those which impact your inner being

words may reveal the self

or words may conceal it

fear works
as it locks against outer interference
from involving the inner self
greed works
as it reaches to grab and grasp unnecessary
external trappings

many questions with few answers
as it should be

———————————— ✄ ————————————

The World is Too Much for Me

This world is too much with me ... late and
  soon. Pardon me please Mr. Wordsworth
For bastardizing your ancient poem
The new world is too much for ME, late and
  soon.
I am bombarded from all sides ...
Now I'm told no Bending, no Lifting no
  Twisting ... NO BLT
Tino does that for me ... No he does that TO
  me twice a week at Agility.
The Covid-19 pandemic is enough for my
  sense of insecurity,
Which I share with the world ... beyond
  borders.
I was already trying to recover from fractured
  vertebrae ... before the virus threatened us
  all.
Under the cover of those clouds I was whisked
  away to the hospital for a quickie gall
  bladder removal by Dr. Kommareddi, a 50
  year old youngster from India.
I finished writing my chapter on Masks.
Everyone started wearing masks ... A trend
  gone viral ... Global?
Two weeks later, I was told I had to have some
  extra fluid removed from somewhere in my
  innards.
"You must be here by 7:00 AM."
I was there ... on time.
Went through the prepping,

Was wheeled into the little tunnel
"Take a deep breath ... Hold it ."
Time passes.
"You may breathe again."
Gee, Thanks!
I do enjoy breathing,
But ever since the coronavirus hovered, I've
    had to limit too close to anyone else. "It
    seems the fluid on your liver has
    diminished, so we won't have to poke
    around in there any more ... Isn't that nice?"
"Well, I don't really appreciate the poking ...
    particularly the interior." So ... I unprep ...
    we go home.
"Oh look! ... Finger Rock is enshrouded in
    smoke."
I had just started breathing again, and now am
    cautioned anew with fresh possibilities of
    breathing smoke ... Not even second hand.
Just the thought, prompts a hacking cough.
I watch the flames come over the Catalinas
filling the crevices with dancing color.
That was before we were told, "Just get ready
    to go."
But I just got back.
I apologize Mr. Eliot,
Fractured vertebrae is the way the world ends.
Raging fire is the way the world ends.
Covid-19 is the way the world ends.
Not with a bang ... but a whimper.
I'm whimpering.

The Mirror

The old codger wandered
seemingly
aimlessly
around the room in what appeared to be a
pattern of searching
searching for what
was a question even he was not prepared
to answer
had he forgotten to dress
this morning
or
was that
yet another act of defiance
of protocol
or
dementia
or simply cussed
orneriness
he wandered naked
past the window
to the mirror
then peeked in
I smiled
he looked somewhat embarrassed

---

examining
me closely
he hurriedly turned to leave
just
as I stepped
out of the frame

An Image

On my black mirror
An image appeared
It seems to be a parachute
Just what I need
A parachute for bailing out.

So I look closer
To learn the details
The ribbing of the cords
The ribbon of the silk.

As I get closer
I don't believe it's a parachute.

It seems to be a mushroom cloud.

Why the mixed message
With colliding images?

It's not the image that's worthwhile
That one must heed.

It's the perception of the image
Appearing darkly
On my screen.
That one must deal with.

What is it you see?
   on the horizon
   or close at hand?
      Time will tell
         And time ain't talkin'.

4.
POETIC
EXPERIMENTS

Though poetry is usually serious writing,
it is often the playful use of words. As the
scientist is careful to use the precise word,
the poet may choose words with a deliberate
range of meanings with implication and
nuance — and then at times with rhyme or
alliteration. Some of these earlier word
choices have been given names: limerick,
haiku, concrete poetry, sonnet, blank verse,
etc.

These last pages will be devoted to playing
with words, inviting the reader to join in the
game.

---- ❧ ----

Given Words

In the Trump administration it was
forbidden for the Center of Diseases to
use these specific words: DIVERSITY,
FETUS, SCIENCE-BASED, TRANSGENDER,
VULNERABLE, ENTITLEMENT, EVIDENCE-
BASED
Thus I used them all together as a rhymed
poem:

Trump's Forbidden Words

The adversity
of DIVERSITY
caused him to cuss
about the FETUS
and was displaced
by the SCIENCE-BASED
provocateur
of the TRANSGENDER,
which failed to enable
the VULNERABLE,
and not content
with ENTITLEMENT
but was faced
with the EVIDENCE-BASED.

Note: Pretty bad doggerel, but fun

Given Phrases

Rather than just single words, I discovered some rather interesting poetic lines in a script, written by a fellow playwright, Gavin Kaynor. I asked him for permission to pull those phrases from his script and use them in a poem. He gave permission. His lines are in caps and mine are basically transitions, in lower case. Even though I had no emotional intention with my words, I merely hoped to make a cogent poetic statement. Some readers have expressed emotional recall in reading the combined lines.

———————— ✗ ————————

A Bit of Insanity in Poetry
A Bit of Poetry in Insanity

WHAT SORT OF MAN WOULD BE BEST
   FORGOTTEN
a senseless question
he's already too forgotten
to remember

words can be rather cruel or glib but it's
EASY TO SAY WHEN IT'S WORDS FROM THE
   HEART
connected HUMANITY DID THAT TO US
bringing you to me or was it me to you
IN MY ARMS YOU'RE AN ANGEL

in my heart, too often
I'M NO ONE WITHOUT A NAME OR A PAST
A DIAGNOSIS WITH NO CURE
NO PLACE OF BIRTH of spiritual birth
searching for A DIVINITY WORTH WORSHIPPING

the urologist has informed me of PROSTATE
   TROUBLE
IT'S NOT ENOUGH TO KNOW I LIKE CARAMEL
   APPLES
or THIS MAN WHO I WAS
THE MAN I'M NOT ABLE TO REMEMBER
but THE GIFT OF MY MEMORY
I recall ONE CAGE FOR ANOTHER

AS OF TODAY
MY MOTHER WEPT
from her body and soul
SHE BECAME YOUR WAY IN

even though
LIFE at times seemed to be A CLOSED BOOK
we always have ANOTHER ACT TO GRIND
THAT'S CALLED PROGRESS
NEARLY BELIEVABLE
WHOEVER wherever YOU ARE
and in what stream you have floated

IF NOT FOR THE VOICES OF HISTORY
It's not enough to know
BALONEY IS NOT A FOOD
or to know WHO I CHOOSE TO BE
is not the person you see

OTHER PEOPLE'S LIVES
complicate our own
to such an extent that
we long to be
the man who wasn't there
when ANONYMITY IS A BLESSING
NEARLY AS GOOD AS MUSTARD GAS

after the trick or treat
SPIRITS old and young SEEK NOURISHMENT
    AND WARMTH
the older ones glimpsing ESSENCES OF
    YESTERDAY

---

the younger ones opening SOMETHING OF MY
    CHILDHOOD

THE NEEDING MAKES IT REAL
even when REGRETS are TRIPPING THEM UP
and the LESSONS STAY WITH US

A NOWHERE MAN
makes it difficult
to pursue HUMAN CONNECTIONS
IT'S ONE PRISON OR ANOTHER with
LOVERS OR OTHER STRANGERS while
SACRIFICIAL LAMBS DIE ON THE ALTAR

UBIQUITY IS NOT THE SAME AS OMNISCIENCE
at least to the MAN WHO DOESN'T EXIST
DESPERATION MAKES FOR STRANGE
    BEDFELLOWS
FALSE MEMORIES COULD BE BETTER THAN NONE
to FEEL THE MOMENT like
BIRDS IN A GRAY SKY
how do we go there
THERE IS HOW YOU GO THERE
just a place to be safe
WHERE IN THE HELL ARE WE EVER SAFE
how can we tell them
PEOPLE ADVERTISE THEMSELVES
feel she's terribly deluded
BETTER HER ILLUSION THAN YOUR REALITY
why do you suppose we're JOINED AT THE PALM
VICTIMS OF EACH OTHER
there's really only

A FINE LINE BETWEEN CREATIVITY AND
    INSANITY
more than ever I'm
ALONE BUT NEVER LONELY
MIRRORS OF WHAT I HAD BECOME

I learned a long time ago
KEEP YOUR HANDS OUTTTA THE COOKIE JAR

I also learned
YOU CAN'T KILL NOBODY
but I do know
SOMEBODY IS DEAD
too often
YOU'RE CONFUSING YOUR REALITIES

I AM THE KEY to my own destiny
but you must
LET THE PAST INFORM THE PRESENT
I learned the hard way to
BEWARE OF WHAT I WISHED FOR
THE LIES WE TELL OURSELVES ... AND ONE
    ANOTHER 'twixt heaven and hell
THE FICTIONS WE MAKE OF OTHER PEOPLE
as we all are somehow
CAUGHT BETWEEN GRACE AND THE GHASTLY
we must remember that we're
NOBODY WITHOUT SOMEBODY

————————— ✕ —————————

Challenging Words

I developed this game to help students remember the meaning of specific words.

Don't you	ABHOR that
public	BIGOT who
is a	COUNTERFEIT of a patriot?
Instead of his willingness to	
	ENFRANCHISE a grant for immigrants.
He would do anything to	
	HAMPER them from any
attempt to	KINDLE an interest in the political process.
His	NOXIOUS attitude is counter
to a	PLACID ambiance one might hope for
newcomers. The	REMUNERATION of peace of mind
was certainly no	TALISMAN for his efforts.

ABHOR - Hate
BIGOT - Biased person
COUNTERFEIT - Fake
ENFRANCHISE - Grant certain legal right
HAMPER - Obstruct
KINDLE -Light a fire
NOXIOUS - Harmful
PLACID - Peaceful

REMUNERATION - Payment
TALISMAN - Lucky Charm
Note: It's now your tum to supply the additional words, linking all these words in a short paragraph.

DEFINITIONS (to be linked)

ABRASIVE - Rough
BILK- Cheat
COVERT - Hidden
ENGENDER - Cause
HANGAR - Large structure
KNOTTY - Complicated
NUANCE - Shade of meaning
PLAGIARISM - Taking credit for someone
    else's work
RENOWN - Fame
TANGENT - Going off the subject

---- ✄ ----

Concrete Poetry

This poetic form is literally the shape of the words on the printed page. Some people have said that these words and phrases don't have to mean anything. I contend the exact opposite. The poetic form should enhance the verbiage. The words of a sonnet have extra depth because of the rhymes and specific number of lines. The intent and tone of the limerick is set by the rhyme scheme and length and beat of each line.

The Limerick

Please permit me to digress a moment to play with the rhythm and beats of the limerick. The rhyme pattern has lines 1,2 and 5 rhyming. Lines 3 and 4 have their own rhymes. Lines 1, 2 and 5 will have three beats each in oral presentation. Lines 3 and 4 have two beats each.

Example:
A mountain boy named Jake
Cut a sapling in order to make
A walking cane,
But it was quite plain
That the stick was only a rake.

The reader has a chance to play with
limericks.

A young lady loved to write
And stayed up half the night.
The shadows did creep
When she fell asleep,

____

There was a smart fellow from Kent
Who went to see the president

____
____
Discovering the funds had been poorly spent

Back to CONCRETE poetry

The Answer

We seek
the answer to
the meaning of life
in the question, itself.
The meaning of life
is to question.

One may trek
Up Baux Mountain
To climb a red oak tree
To sit on a limb and meditate
As the sun behind Pilot Mountain
sinks slowly, ever so slowly
but it is moving, until it
pops suddenly out of
sight, completely.

Then it's quiet
Everything is static
nirvana, momentarily.

As the light dims
evening sounds begin
The night critters emerge
from their ponds and burrows,
new yet ancient
nocturnal
actively seeking home.

Yet.
Honestly to
question, not
just a contention
for attention
intentionally
is to live.

Active.
and alive.
one may trod
up to Machu Picchu
and question the Incas
Why were you ever here?
What prompted you to leave?
We hope that the questions
Will never be completely
answered; for it's like
the end of a puzzle
when the mystery
the final answer
is discovered
the action
is over
Static.

When
the game
is over all you
need is the score,
but you want to watch the
hurrahs of the game to
earn the quietude of
knowing the game
final score
When
You look
For a lost item
And have found it
why would you
look any
further?

Not true
with the search
for an answer to the
meaning of life which is the
quest, itself.

Mamma on a Greyhound Bus

Mamma had a thing with Greyhound buses.
As I think more on it a ride
on a Greyhound bus
was her sense of heaven.
If she could get on a Greyhound bus,
it didn't matter so much where she was going.
But she was going, usually with a mission
To visit someone in the family
Needing her care.

Preparing
for the trip,
she approached
the ticket window.
Unclasping her faded
silk purse, she retrieved
a roll of dollar bills, which
she had saved by trimming the
grocery budget a little each
week. I wouldn't call it
deception, for after
all, she had some
needs too.

Obtaining
the ticket, she
clutched it close
 to her heart, then
behind a short line
of people, she handed
the ticket to the driver, as
she gave him a benign smile.

She boarded the bus and
quickly found a window
seat on the right side
of the bus.

However
she couldn't
get her traveling
bag up on the overhead
luggage rack too far over
the head of this little woman
for her to reach and deposit her
bag there. This woman had birthed
and tended babies, cooked on primitive
woodstoves, scrubbed clothes on
ridged washboards but couldn't
always reach the requirements
of this outer world. If she
could only have been
a little taller.

So
she
seated
herself in
the window
seat, put her
quilted traveling
bag in the seat beside
her, realizing that
she'd have to
give up the
extra seat,
if another
rider may
need it.

She
carefully
took off her
hat, examined
its appearance,
straightened the stems
of the little blue flowers.
She decided to wear it
a bit longer, so
she put it
on again.

As
soon
as she
was settled in
her seat, she
was on her way.
Even before the
bus had pulled out
of the terminal tunnel
under the Robert E. Lee
Hotel In Winston,
heaven couldn't
be lovelier
Than
This.
In
the
terminal
the noise from
the buses reverberated
off the tunnel concrete walls

---

with deafening power...
her personal
power to be
herself.
On
one
of her
bus trips,
she was going
with my sister, Della Sue,
to straighten out some misunderstanding
with her instructor at the nurse training school
at the Presbyterian Hospital in Charlotte.
After completing that mission
she headed back home
alone to take up her
normal life of daily
responsibilities.
Those responsibilities
for family were awesome
out beyond the power and
phone lines, past the end
of the paved road.

She was,
during the ride,
completely non-responsible.
Not to mean that she ever shirked
her responsibilities. However no one
could then expect anything of her.
While on the bus she was
incommunicado.

On another trip,
she was headed to Wisconsin
to see her three granddaughters, her son
and daughter-in-law.
She planned the trip carefully.
She had to transfer buses in Charleston, WV.
She had a nephew in Charleston.
So her plan was to call him.
Being family, held some value
in her belief world. She would call
to say hello and tell of her bus transfer.
He would volunteer to come to pick her up and
    take her home
to spend the night, even if that meant sleeping
    on a pallet on the floor.
She made the call told him of her schedule.
She listened carefully to his response,
which didn't contain an invitation
to spend the night. She spent
the night in the bus depot.
It wasn't the bus, but
she knew the bus
would be there
in the morning.

Meanwhile,
she observed and
listened to everything
around her. She was too
shy to strike up a conversation
with any other bus travelers.
She could listen, thus,
knowing her fellow
travelers a little
bit better.

Once when she visited,
she had a terrible headache.
"Was the noise too much, Mamma?"
"No the noise was okay.
I just couldn't understand."
"Couldn't understand what?"
"The couple seated in front of me
were talking a foreign language.
Just jabbering and jabbering.
I listened carefully but couldn't
understand a word they were saying.
It gave me a headache."

Her last bus ride was in '68.
She took the bus to visit us that year.
It was Christmas, and she had
such a wonderful time with
her granddaughters that
she announced,
"From now on I'm going
to spend every Christmas with you
and Luan and the girls, no matter where
you all may be living. The
Greyhound bus
will get me
there."

Mamma didn't make it to another Christmas.

She was killed
in a traffic accident
in a pick-up truck.

Would she have been safe
on a greyhound bus?

Learning to Drive

I had learned to drive
before we moved beyond the paved roads.
It was 1935, when I got a Red Racer for Christmas.
I had never driven before but I was determined
To learn before summer came when
I would be able to drive outside

I should mention that
Christmas I had just
celebrated in
November
My fifth
Birthday

The little Red Racer
Was fueled by pedal power
Plus there was no power steering
My roadway was in a circle always turning
Right through the doorways in the little white
house

Once I got it started,
Which was a chore itself
Then the next problem was
Continuing the forward momentum
Without mistakenly lurching backward

Once that pedal
Procedure was mastered
It was imperative to keep the

Steering engaged in a proper
Manner to avoid the road blocks
Which actually were the door
Jambs shared by the four
Rooms forming a large

Cube connecting the four
Smaller cubes (rooms)
Forming a perfect circle for
A sleek red racecar, always
Turning right in that circle

I even learned to turn
Around in one of the rooms
Heading back in the other direction
But hoping that I wasn't going the
wrong way and might meet oncoming traffic
and driving in the wrong lane

But the freeway was clear
No other traffic near
But the marks left
On the door jambs
Are probably still there after many
And many
A year

We moved after that so may times
That somewhere the little red
Racer had been
Left some how
Behind

My next vehicle to learn to drive
Had pedals but only two wheels
Handle bars but no
Steering
Wheel
We had no
Money to buy
a bike

So at the
Age of eleven
I learned to stay upright
On someone else's
Two-wheel bike
When I was fifteen I
got my very own bicycle
Which I rode joyfully over
Washboard ridges on
Our sand-clay road
Out beyond even
Any paved
Roads
At fourteen
I learned quickly
How to drive a team
Of huge draft horses
Pulling logs up hills
And out of ravines

It was that year also that
I learned to drive a doodlebug tractor
Which was an amalgam of a '33 Chevy
With a truck rear end
Four on the floor

Gear shift
A similar problem
With the little Red Racer
To keep it going forward until
I had learned its pedals
Properly
With the doodlebug
It was the gear shift stick
Forming an H with my
Right hand
Clutch then starting off low
The lower left of the gear stick
Then as casually as possible
Clutch again, as I'd throw
that gear shift
Up into second

Instead the blamed thing
Shifted into reverse
Lurching me and
The vehicle
Backward down the lane

Not fatally affecting me
Nor breaking the gears
Out of commission
Like the little red race car
Until I learned the appropriate
Proper procedure

In my 80s driving a grown-up car
It wasn't reverse this time but
Instead it lurched forward
Scratching a lady's rear...

Rear bumper
I should Say

So,
Goodbye

Car key, car,
And driving
Privileges

Now several years
After the little Red Racer
I'm learning anew to
Drive a four-wheeler.

But alas it's sad to say that
Like the little red racer
The wheel chair is
leaving its marks
On the door jambs
Eighty-five
years
later

And so it goes

As we wheel our way
Through hollows and ridges
We leave
Our marks
On the door jambs
Of life